Helicopter

Oral Exam Guide

by Ryan Dale

When used with the Oral Exam Guides, this book prepares you for the oral portion of the Private, Instrument, Commercial, Flight Instructor, or ATP helicopter checkride.

Aviation Supplies & Academics, Inc.
Newcastle, Washington

Helicopter Oral Exam Guide
Helicopter Supplement for the Oral Exam Guides
by Ryan Dale

(Based on the Oral Exam Guide Series by Michael D. Hayes.)

Aviation Supplies & Academics, Inc.
7005 132nd Place SE
Newcastle, Washington 98059-3153

Visit the ASA website often (**www.asa2fly.com**, Product Updates link)
to find updates posted there due to FAA regulation revisions that may
affect this book.

Printed in the United States of America

09   08   07   06   9   8   7   6   5   4   3   2   1

ASA-OEG-H
ISBN   1-56027-608-8
       978-1-56027-608-1

Library of Congress Cataloging-in-Publication Data:

Dale, Ryan.
  Helicopter oral exam guide / by Ryan Dale.— 1st ed.
      p.   cm.
  "When used with the Oral Exam Guides, this book prepares you for the oral portion of
the Private, Instrument, Commercial, Flight Instructor, or ATP helicopter checkride."
  ISBN-13: 978-1-56027-608-1 (pbk.)
  ISBN-10: 1-56027-608-8 (pbk.)
  1. Helicopters—Piloting—Examinations—Study guides. 2. Helicopters—
Piloting—Examinations, questions, etc. I. Title.

  TL716.5.D35 2006
  629.132'5252076—dc22
                          2006001953

Contents

Continued

Instrument Rating

Commercial Pilot

Certified Flight Instructor

Introduction
How to Use This Book

This *Helicopter Oral Exam Guide* is designed for pilots who are involved with helicopter training, and complements the *Oral Exam Guides* by Michael Hayes. It provides information specific to helicopter operations, preparing you for the oral questioning portion of the FAA practical exam (also called "checkride"). This book should be used along with the *Oral Exam Guides* by Michael Hayes, which focus on airplane operations. This book is designed to provide you with an additional resource to help you on the path to becoming a professional helicopter pilot.

Questions and answers are organized into five sections, one for each certificate or rating sought. Each certificate or rating requires the knowledge of the previous sections as well. So, to prepare for the certified flight instructor, you should also read the private and commercial sections.

At the end of this book, there are two sections intended to be used as a quick reference guide for the Practical Test Standards (PTS) for private, instrument, and commercial ratings. The Airline Transport Pilot (ATP) rating uses PTS from both the instrument and commercial ratings. The reference to POH in the private, instrument, commercial, and CFI ratings refers to a Robinson R-22 helicopter. In the ATP rating the RFM (Rotorcraft Flight Manual) refers to a Bell 206B3 helicopter; however, this guide does not take the place of the POH or RFM for which your flight will take place.

Begin your studies by referring to the *Oral Exam Guide* by Michael Hayes for the certificate or rating you're working on. Below is a list of questions to disregard when reading these books, when preparing for a helicopter rating. Then continue your studies using the questions in this book. Using the books together in this way, you will be completely prepared for your helicopter checkride.

Ryan Dale

Disregard the following questions from the *Oral Exam Guides* by Michael Hayes while preparing for your helicopter tests:

	Chapter	Section	Questions
Private Pilot	1	B	3–5
(ASA-OEG-P)	3	A	11, 15–17, 20–27
	3	B	3–6
	3	C	2–5
	4	A	1–7
	5	D	12
Instrument Rating	1	A	1
(ASA-OEG-I)	1	D	6
	1	F	10
	2	C	1
	4	D	8
Commercial Pilot	1	A	16, 19
(ASA-OEG-C)	1	C	6
	3	B	All
	3	I	13
	3	J	All
	4	A	All
	4	D	All
	4	E	All
	4	H	All
	4	K	2
	4	O	6–8
	4	P–R	All
	5	A	10, 11, 13–18
	5	B	4–6, 11, 14, 17–20
	5	C	All
	6	C	1, 3
	9	All	All
Certified Flight Instructor	3	C, D, E, L	All
(ASA-OEG-CFI)	4–10	All	All
Airline Transport Pilot	1	B	All
(ASA-OEG-ATP)			

This book may be supplemented with other comprehensive study materials as noted in parentheses after each question. For example: (FAA-H-8083-25). The abbreviations for these materials and their titles are listed below. Be sure to use the latest revision of these references when reviewing for the test.

14 CFR Part 1	*Definitions and Abbreviations*
14 CFR Part 61	*Certification: Pilots, Flight Instructors, and Ground Instructors*
14 CFR Part 91	*General Operating and Flight Rules*
14 CFR Part 97	*Standard Instrument Approach Procedures*
14 CFR Part 133	*Rotorcraft External-Load Operations*
14 CFR Part 135	*Operating Requirements: Commuter and On-Demand Operations and Rules Governing Persons On Board Such Aircraft*
AC 65-15	*A&P Mechanic Airframe Handbook*
AFM	*FAA-Approved Rotorcraft Flight Manual*
AIM	*Aeronautical Information Manual*
ASA-PHF	*Principles of Helicopter Flight* by Walter Wagtendonk
FAA-H-8081-7	*Flight Instructor Rotorcraft Practical Test Standards*
FAA-H-8081-15	*Private Pilot Rotorcraft Practical Test Standards*
FAA-H-8081-16	*Commercial Pilot Rotorcraft Practical Test Standards*
FAA-H-8083-1	*Aircraft Weight & Balance Handbook*
FAA-H-8083-21	*Rotorcraft Flying Handbook*
FAA-H-8083-25	*Pilot's Handbook of Aeronautical Knowledge*
POH	*Pilot Operating Handbook* (be sure to reference the one specific to the helicopter you'll be flying for the checkride)

Helicopter Operations:
Private Pilot

Certificates and Documents

1

1. What kind of helicopters can you fly with a private pilot certificate? (14 CFR 61.31)

Any helicopter up to 12,500 pounds, except for the R-22 and R-44 unless the SFAR 73 to Part 61 is followed.

2. Can you fly a twin turbine powered helicopter? (14 CFR 61.31)

Yes. You can fly any helicopter up to 12,500 pounds, except for the R-22 and R-44 (unless you meet the requirements outlined in SFAR 73 to Part 61).

3. If you take your flight review in a Bell 206, can you act as PIC in the R-22? (SFAR No. 73 to Part 61)

No, according to SFAR No. 73 2(c)(1): No flight review completed to satisfy 61.56...shall be valid for the operation of the R-22 helicopter *unless* that flight review was taken in an R-22.

4. To act as PIC in the R-22 how often do you have to take a flight review if you have less than 200 hours? (SFAR No. 73 to Part 61)

According to SFAR No. 73 2(b)(1), every 12 calendar months and have obtained an endorsement for that flight review from a certified flight instructor authorized under paragraph (b)(5).

The review must include:

a. Enhanced training in autorotation procedures,

b. Engine Rotor RPM control without the use of the governor,

c. Low rotor RPM recognition and recovery, and

d. Effects of low G maneuvers and proper recovery procedures.

Cross-Country Flight Planning

2

1. What types of charts are available for use in helicopter VFR navigation? (FAA-H-8083-25)

WAC—World Aeronautical Charts, revised annually except several Alaskan Charts and the Mexican/Caribbean charts, which are revised every 2 years. Not good for low altitude or slow flight because of scale.

Sectionals—Sectional Charts, these charts are revised semiannually except for some areas outside the coterminous United States where they are revised annually.

Terminals—VFR Terminal Area Charts, helpful when flying in or near Class B airspace, these charts are revised semiannually, except for several Alaskan and Caribbean Charts.

Helicopter Route Charts—These three-color charts depict current aeronautical information useful to helicopter pilots navigating in areas with high concentrations of helicopter activity. They are not updated on a regular basis because they will be updated when a significant number of changes have accumulated, or when safety related or major airspace modifications warrant the printing of a new chart.

2. How low can helicopter pilots fly? (14 CFR 91.119)

Helicopters may be operated at less than the minimums prescribed in paragraph (b) or (c) of this section if the operation is conducted *without hazard to persons or property* on the surface. In addition, each person operating a helicopter shall comply with any routes or altitudes specifically prescribed for helicopters by the FAA.

3. When flying into an airport environment, what rules apply to helicopters? (14 CFR 91.126)

Each pilot of a helicopter must avoid the flow of fixed-wing aircraft.

4. What are the VFR weather minimums for Class G airspace below 1,200 feet AGL? (14 CFR 91.155)

A helicopter may be operated *clear of clouds* if operated at a speed that allows the pilot adequate opportunity to see any air traffic or obstruction in time to avoid a collision.

5. What is required for a helicopter pilot to obtain a "Special VFR at a controlled airport"? (14 CFR 91.157)

Special VFR operations may only be conducted—

a. With an ATC clearance;

b. Clear of clouds

6. What are the fuel requirements for helicopters under VFR flight rules? (14 CFR Part 91.151)

No person may begin a flight in a rotorcraft under VFR conditions unless (considering wind and forecast weather conditions) there is enough fuel to fly to the first point of intended landing and, assuming normal cruising speed, to fly after that for at least 20 minutes.

Performance and Limitations

3

A. Aerodynamics

1. What is the center of pressure? (FAA-H-8083-21)

Center of pressure is the imaginary point on the chord line where the resultants of all aerodynamic forces are considered to be concentrated. When the center of pressure lifting force is behind the pivot point on a rotor blade, it tends to cause the rotor disc to pitch up. As the angle of attack increases, the center of pressure moves forward. If it moves ahead of the pivot point, the pitch of the rotor disc decreases. Since the angle of attack of the rotor blades is constantly changing during each cycle of rotation, the asymmetrical blades of the helicopter tend to flap, feather, lead, and lag to a greater degree.

2. What is the axis of rotation? (FAA-H-8083-21)

The axis of rotation is an imaginary line about which the rotor rotates. It is represented by a line drawn through the center of, and perpendicular to, the tip-path plane.

3. What is the rotor tip path plane? (FAA-H-8083-21)

The tip-path plane is the imaginary circular plane outlined by the rotor blade tips as they make a cycle of rotation.

4. What is the blade pitch angle? (FAA-H-8083-21)

The pitch angle of a rotor blade is the angle between its chord line and the reference plane containing the rotor hub. You control the pitch angle of the blades with the flight controls.

The *collective pitch* changes each rotor blade an equal amount of pitch no matter where it is located in the plane of rotation (rotor disc) and is used to change rotor thrust.

Continued

The *cyclic pitch* control changes the pitch of each blade as a function of where it is in the plane of rotation. This allows for trimming the helicopter in pitch and roll during forward flight and for maneuvering in all flight conditions.

5. What is magnus effect? (FAA-H-8083-21)

Looking at a cylinder rotating in an air stream, the top surface area is rotating in the same direction as the airflow; the local velocity at the surface is high on top and low on the bottom. The difference in surface velocity accounts for a difference in pressure, with the pressure being lower on the top than the bottom. This low-pressure area produces an upward force known as the "magnus effect."

6. What is Newton's Third Law? (FAA-H-8083-21)

"For every action there is an equal and opposite reaction." The air that is deflected downward also produces an upward (lifting) reaction.

7. Why does the helicopter drift in the same direction as the anti-torque rotor thrust? (FAA-H-8083-21)

The helicopter drifts in the same direction as the anti-torque rotor thrust due to translating tendency.

8. What is translating tendency? (FAA-H-8083-21, ASA-PHF)

During hovering flight, a single main rotor helicopter tends to drift in the same direction as anti-torque rotor thrust. Some designers incorporate methods that automatically correct for tail rotor drift. Most common types are either tilting the rotor mast opposite the drift and the use of a "bias" in the cyclic control mechanism that holds the cyclic stick slightly to the left.

"Translating tendency occurs anytime in flight when power is in use; it must be corrected. In forward flight and especially at speeds approaching cruise speed or higher, the directional stability of the aircraft reduces the requirement for anti-torque so that tail rotor drift becomes less significant."

—W.J. Wagtendonk, *Principles of Helicopter Flight*

9. What is pendular action? (FAA-H-8083-21)

Since the fuselage of the helicopter, with a single main rotor, is suspended from a single point and has considerable mass, it is free to oscillate either longitudinally or laterally in the same way as a pendulum. This pendular action can be exaggerated by over controlling; therefore, control movements should be smooth and not exaggerated.

10. What is coning? (FAA-H-8083-21)

As a vertical takeoff is made, two major forces are acting at the same time—

Centrifugal force acting outward and perpendicular to the rotor mast,

Lift acting upward and parallel to the mast.

The result of these two forces is that the blades assume a conical path instead of remaining in the plane perpendicular to the mast.

11. What is Coriolis effect? (FAA-H-8083-21)

When a rotor blade flaps upward, the *center of mass* of that blade moves *closer to the axis of rotation* and blade acceleration takes place in order to conserve angular momentum.

12. What is ground effect? (FAA-H-8083-21)

Ground effect usually occurs less than one rotor diameter above the surface. As the induced airflow through the rotor disc is reduced by the surface friction, the lift vector increases. This allows a lower rotor blade angle for the same amount of lift, which reduces induced drag.

13. What is blade flapping? (FAA-H-8083-21)

Blade flapping is the ability of the rotor blade to move up, or down, in a vertical direction. Lift, acting upward and parallel to the mast, causes the blades to flap upwards. Blades may flap independently or in unison to help compensate for dissymmetry of lift.

14. What is dissymmetry of lift? (FAA-H-8083-21)

When the helicopter moves through the air, the relative airflow through the main rotor disc is different on the advancing side than on the retreating side. The relative wind encountered by the advancing blade is increased by the forward speed of the helicopter, while the relative wind speed, acting on the retreating blade, is reduced by the helicopter's forward airspeed. Therefore, because of the relative wind speed, the advancing blade side of the rotor disc produces more lift than the retreating blade side.

15. What is low RPM blade stall? (POH)

Power available from the engine is directly proportional to RPM. If the PRM drops 10%, there is 10% less power. With less power, the helicopter will start to settle, and if the collective is raised to stop it from settling, the RPM will be pulled down even lower, causing the ship to settle even faster. If the Pilot not only fails to lower collective, but also pulls up on the collective to keep the ship from going down, the rotor will stall almost immediately. When it stalls, the blades will both "blow-back" and cut off the tail cone, or it will just stop flying, allowing the helicopter to fall at an extreme rate, while the blades flap up. In either case, the resulting crash is likely to be fatal.

16. What is effective translational lift? (FAA-H-8083-21)

Effective translational lift is the additional lift obtained when entering forward flight, due to the increased efficiency of the rotor system. As the helicopter accelerates through this speed, the rotor moves out of its vortices and is in relatively undisturbed air. The airflow is also now more horizontal, which reduces induced flow and drag with a corresponding increase in angle of attack and lift.

17. What is transverse flow effect? (FAA-H-8083-21)

As the helicopter accelerates in forward flight, induced flow drops to near zero at the forward disc area and increases at the aft disc area. This increases the angle of attack at the front disc area causing the rotor blade to flap up, and reduces angle of attack at the aft disc area causing the rotor blade to flap down. The result is a tendency for the helicopter to roll slightly to the right as it accelerates through approximately 20 knots or if the headwind is approximately 20 knots.

18. **Explain gyroscopic precession.** (FAA-H-8083-21)

The spinning main rotor of a helicopter acts like a gyroscope. As such, it has the properties of gyroscopic action, one of which is precession. Precession happens when you apply a force to one side of a spinning disk—that force gets transferred 90 degrees ahead of where it was applied, in the direction of rotation.

B. Weight and Balance

1. **Define the following weight and balance terms:**
(FAA-H-8083-21)

Arm—The horizontal distance from the datum to any component of the helicopter or to any object located within the helicopter.

Basic Empty Weight—The starting point for weight computations is the basic empty weight, which is the weight of the standard helicopter, optional equipment, unusable fuel, and full operating fluids including full engine oil.

Maximum Gross Weight—The maximum weight of the helicopter. Most helicopters have an internal maximum gross weight, which refers to the weight within the helicopter structure and an external maximum gross weight, which refers to the weight of the helicopter with an external load.

2. **What performance characteristics will be adversely affected when a helicopter is overloaded?**
(FAA-H-8083-1)

a. Longer takeoff run.

b. Both the rate and angle of climb will be reduced.

c. The service ceiling will be lowered.

d. The cruising speed will be reduced.

e. The cruising range will be shortened.

f. Maneuverability will be decreased.

Continued

   g. A longer landing run will be required because the landing speed will be higher.

   h. Excessive loads will be imposed on the structure, especially the landing gear.

Note: Operation above maximum weight could result in structural deformation or failure during flight if you encounter:

- Excessive load factors
- Strong wind gusts
- Turbulence

3. What performance characteristics will be adversely affected when a helicopter is underloaded? (FAA-H-8083-1)

Operation below the minimum weight could adversely affect the handling characteristics of the helicopter during autorotations.

   a. Operations under the minimum weight may not reach desirable rotor RPM during autorotations.

   b. Forward ballasts are used to help compensate single pilot operations.

4. What effect does a forward center of gravity have on helicopter flight characteristics? (FAA-H-8083-1)

There may not be enough cyclic authority to allow the helicopter to flare for a landing, and it will consequently require an excessive landing distance.

5. What effect does a rearward center of gravity have on helicopter flight characteristics? (FAA-H-8083-1)

There might not be enough cyclic power to prevent the tail boom striking the ground. If gusty winds should cause the helicopter to pitch up during high-speed flight, there might not be enough forward cyclic control to lower the nose.

C. Retreating Blade Stall

1. What is retreating blade stall? (FAA-H-8083-21)

To generate the same amount of lift across the rotor disc, the advancing blade flaps up while the retreating blade flaps down. This causes the angle of attack to decrease on the advancing blade, which reduces lift, and increase on the retreating blade, which increases lift. As the forward speed increases, at some point the low blade speed on the retreating blade, together with its high angle of attack, causes a loss of lift (stall).

2. How does retreating blade stall affect helicopter performance? (FAA-H-8083-21)

Retreating blade stall is a major factor in limiting a helicopter's top forward speed (V_{NE}).

3. What conditions are conducive to retreating blade stall? (FAA-H-8083-21)

High weight, low rotor RPM, high-density altitude, turbulence and/or steep, abrupt turns are all conducive to retreating blade stall at high forward airspeeds.

D. Height/Velocity Diagram

1. What is the height/velocity diagram? (FAA-H-8083-21)

A height/velocity (H/V) diagram, published by the manufacturer for each model of helicopter, depicts the critical combinations of airspeed and altitude should an engine failure occur.

2. Why is the H/V diagram important? (FAA-H-8083-21)

Because your recognition of an engine failure will most likely coincide with, or shortly occur after, ground contact. Even if you detect an engine failure, there may not be sufficient time to rotate the helicopter from a nose low, high airspeed attitude to one suitable for slowing, then landing. Additionally, the altitude loss that occurs during recognition of engine failure and rotation to a landing attitude, may not leave enough altitude to prevent the tail skid from hitting the ground during the landing maneuver.

3. Why is there a lower shaded area of the H/V diagram?
(FAA-H-8083-21)

Even if you detect an engine failure, there may not be sufficient
time to rotate the helicopter from a nose low, high airspeed attitude
to one suitable for slowing, then landing. Additionally, the altitude
loss that occurs during recognition of engine failure and rotation to
a landing attitude, may not leave enough altitude to prevent the tail
skid from hitting the ground during the landing maneuver.

E. Operating Limitations

**1. What factors affect the performance of an aircraft during
takeoffs and landings?** (FAA-H-8083-21)

- Air density (density altitude)
- Surface winds
- Surface conditions (pavement, water, grass, snow)
- Weight

2. How does air density affect helicopter performance?
(FAA-H-8083-25)

The density of air directly affects:
- Efficiency of the rotor blades
- Power output of the engine
- Drag produced by the increased angle of attack
- The amount of lift produced by the main rotor blades
- The efficiency of the tail rotor

3. What effect does wind have on aircraft performance?
(FAA-H-8083-21)

If the helicopter is taking off into the wind, the helicopter will
reach effective translational lift (ETL) sooner; if the helicopter is
taking off downwind ETL will be reached later. If taking off downwind, keep in mind that the helicopter's ground run will be longer
than normal.

4. What is MCP? (POH)

Maximum continuous power.

5. What are some considerations for a crosswind takeoff? (FAA-H-8083-21)

If the takeoff is made during crosswind conditions, the helicopter is flown in a slip during the early stages of the maneuver. The cyclic is held into the wind a sufficient amount to maintain the desired ground track for the takeoff. The heading is maintained with the use of the anti-torque pedals. In other words, the rotor is tilted into the wind so that the sideward movement of the helicopter is just enough to counteract the crosswind effect. To prevent the nose from turning in the direction of the rotor tilt, it is necessary to increase the anti-torque pedal pressure on the side opposite the rotor tilt. After approximately 50 feet of altitude is gained, the helicopter is turned into the wind to maintain the desired ground track. This is called crabbing into the wind. The stronger the crosswind, the more you have to turn the helicopter into the wind to maintain the desired ground track.

6. What is a "5 minute takeoff rating"? (14 CFR 1.1)

Rated takeoff power, with respect to reciprocating, turbopropeller, and turboshaft engine type certification, means the approved brake horsepower that is developed statically under standard sea level conditions, within the engine operating limitations established under Part 33, and limited in use to periods of not over 5 minutes for takeoff operation.

7. What is the correct procedure after pulling the maximum rated takeoff power for five minutes?

Lower power to MCP; inspect engine instruments for higher than normal temperatures and/or pressures.

8. What is V_{NE} below 3,000 feet for the R-22? (POH)

102 KIAS.

9. What is the surface wind and gust spread limit until you have 200 hours in a helicopter and 50 hours in the R-22? (POH)

Flight when surface winds exceed 25 knots, including gusts is prohibited.

Flight when surface wind gust spreads exceed 15 knots is prohibited.

Continued flight in moderate, severe, or extreme turbulence is prohibited.

Additional Study Questions

4

The following questions are designed to provide pilots with a general review of the basic information that a pilot should know about their specific helicopter before taking a flight review or a checkride.

1. What is the normal takeoff speed? _____

2. What is the normal climb speed? _____

3. What is the normal cruise speed? _____

4. What is the best rate of climb speed? _____

5. What is the maximum range speed? _____

6. What is the autorotative descent speed? _____

7. What is the maximum glide speed (autorotations)?
   _____

8. What is the minimum rate of descent speed (autorotations)? _____

9. What is the V_{NE} speed? _____

10. What is the recommended hovering altitude? _____

    What is the green arc for rotor RPM? _____

11. What are the manifold pressure limits? _____

12. What are the cylinder head temperature limits? _____

    What is the make and model of the engine?
    _____

13. **How much horsepower does the engine produce?**

   _____

14. **What is the minimum weight?** _____

15. **What is the maximum weight?** _____

16. **What is the maximum weight limit per seat?** _____

17. **How many usable gallons of fuel can you carry?** _____

18. **Where are the different tanks located and what are their capacities?** _____

19. **Where are the fuel tanks vented?** _____

   What kind of fuel can you use? _____

20. **Where are the sump drains located?** _____

21. **What are the minimum and maximum oil capacities?**

   _____

22. **What is the maximum oil temperature and pressure?**

   _____

23. **What kind of landing gear does the helicopter have?**

   _____

24. **What kind of rotor brake does your aircraft have?**

   _____

   How many people can you carry?

   _____

25. **What is the maximum useful load?** _____

26. **What is the OGE hover capability at max gross weight and +20°C?** _____

27. **What is the IGE hover capability at max gross weight and +20°C?** _____

Helicopter Systems

5

A. Flight Controls

1. What are the four main controls? (FAA-H-8083-21)

Collective pitch control—Changes the pitch angle of all main rotor blades simultaneously, or collectively.

Throttle control—The function of the throttle is to regulate engine RPM Twisting the throttle outboard increases RPM; twisting it inboard decreases RPM.

Cyclic pitch control—Tilts the main rotor disc by changing the pitch angle of the rotor blades in their cycle of rotation. When the main rotor disc is tilted, the horizontal component of lift moves the helicopter in the direction of tilt.

Anti-torque pedals—Control the pitch of the tail rotor blades, and therefore the thrust of the blades.

2. How are the various flight controls operated? (AFM)

These are controlled through a series of mechanical linkages, usually push–pull tubes and bell cranks either with or without hydraulic assist. Some tail rotor pitch change links are operated through a cable system, but in most helicopters, they are a series of push pull tubes, linked by bell cranks.

3. What does the correlator do? (AFM)

A correlator is a mechanical connection between the collective lever and the engine throttle. When the collective lever is raised, power is automatically increased and when lowered, power is decreased. This system maintains RPM close to the desired value, but still requires adjustment of the throttle for fine-tuning.

4. What does the governor do? (AFM)

A governor is a sensing device that senses rotor and engine RPM and makes the necessary adjustments in order to keep rotor RPM constant. In normal operations, once the rotor RPM is set, the *governor* keeps the RPM constant, and there is no need to make any throttle adjustments. Governors are common on all turbine helicopters and used on some piston-powered helicopters.

5. Where is the rotor break located, and how does it work? (AFM)

The rotor brake is mounted on the aft end of the main gearbox and actuated by a cable connected to a pull handle located above and behind the pilot's left shoulder. When the handle is pulled, the leverage actuates drum-like brake pads on the spinning shaft just aft of the main gearbox.

B. Powerplant

1. What type of engine does your aircraft have? (AFM)

A four-cylinder, horizontally opposed, direct-drive, air cooled, carbureted, normally aspirated. Manufactured by Lycoming and rated either at 160 or 145 BHP.

2. What is carburetor heat? (FAA-H-8083-25)

Carburetor heat is an anti-icing system that preheats the air before it reaches the carburetor.

3. How does carburetor heat affect the helicopter? (FAA-H-8083-21)

Carburetor heat is intended to keep the fuel/air mixture above the freezing temperature to prevent the formation of carburetor ice. Carburetor heat can be used to melt ice that has already formed in the carburetor if the accumulation is not too great.

4. Do you adjust the mixture control during flight? (AFM)

The mixture may be leaned for "high" altitude conditions, however during normal operations, the mixture control should not be adjusted because it may result in sudden and complete engine stoppage.

If mixture control is leaned at high altitude, be sure it is pushed back in before descending to lower altitude otherwise the engine may quit.

C. Main Rotor, Anti-Torque Rotor, and Transmission

1. How is the power transferred from the engine to main rotor? (AFM)

A V-belt sheave is bolted directly to the output shaft of the engine. V-belts transmit power to the upper sheave which has an overrunning clutch contained in its hub. The inner shaft of the clutch transmits power forward to the main rotor and aft to the tail rotor. Flexible couplings are located at the input to the main gearbox and at each end of the long tail rotor drive shaft.

2. What is the clutch actuator? (AFM)

After the engine is started, it is coupled to the rotor drive system through V-belts, which are tensioned by raising the upper drive sheave. An electric actuator, located between the two drive sheaves, raises the upper sheave when the pilot engages the clutch switch. The actuator senses the compressive load (belt tension) and switches off when the V-belts are tensioned to the prescribed value. A caution light on the panel is on whenever the actuator is operating, either engaging, or disengaging, or re-tensioning the belts.

3. What are the characteristics of the fully articulated rotor system? (FAA-H-8083-21)

A fully articulated rotor system usually consists of three or more rotor blades. The blades are allowed *to flap, feather,* and *lead* or *lag* independently of each other. Each rotor blade is attached to the rotor hub by a horizontal hinge, called the flapping hinge, which permits the blades to flap up and down. Each blade can move up and down independently of the others. The flapping hinge may be located at varying distances from the rotor hub, and there may be more than one.

4. What are the characteristics of the semi-rigid rotor system? (FAA-H-8083-21)

A semi-rigid rotor system allows for two different movements, *flapping* and *feathering*. This system is normally comprised of two blades, which are rigidly attached to the rotor hub. The hub is then attached to the rotor mast by a trunnion bearing or teetering hinge. This allows the blades to seesaw or flap together. As one blade flaps down, the other flaps up. Feathering is accomplished by the feathering hinge, which changes the pitch angle of the blade.

5. What are the characteristics of the rigid rotor system? (FAA-H-8083-21)

The rigid rotor system is mechanically simple, but structurally complex because operating loads must be absorbed in bending rather than through hinges. In this system, the blades *cannot* flap or lead and lag, but they can be *feathered*.

D. Landing Gear

1. What are the different types of landing gear available to helicopters? (FAA-H-8083-21)

The most common landing gear is a *skid* type gear, which is suitable for landing on various types of surfaces. Some types of skid gear are equipped with dampers so touchdown shocks or jolts are not transmitted to the main rotor system. Landing skids may be fitted with replaceable heavy-duty skid shoes to protect them from excessive wear and tear.

Helicopters can also be equipped with *floats* for water operations, or skis for landing on snow or soft terrain.

Wheels are another type of landing gear. They may be in a tricycle or four-point configuration. Normally, the nose or tail gear is free to swivel as the helicopter is taxied on the ground.

2. Describe the type of landing gear on this helicopter. (AFM)

A spring and yield skid-type landing gear is used. The gear will absorb most hard landings elastically. However, in an extremely hard landing, the struts will hinge up and outward as the center cross tube yields (takes permanent set) to absorb the impact. Hardened steel wear shoes are located on the bottom of each skid.

3. How do you control the helicopter during a surface taxi? (FAA-H-8083-21)

The cyclic—Maintains ground track.

The collective—Controls starting, stopping, and speed while taxiing.

Anti-torque pedals—Maintains heading of the helicopter.

For those helicopters with wheels, a surface taxi is used whenever you wish to minimize the effects of rotor downwash.

E. Fuel, Oil, and Hydraulic

1. What kind of fuel system do you have on your helicopter? (AFM)

The fuel system is gravity-flow (no fuel pumps) and includes a fuel tank, a shut-off valve in the cabin behind the left seat, and a fuel strainer. The air vent is located inside the mast fairing above the fuel tank. The optional auxiliary tank is interconnected with the main tank so one valve controls the flow from both tanks.

2. How can you check for water, sediment, and fuel type/grade in the tanks?

A tank drain is located at the forward left side of the tank and is actuated by pushing in on the extended tube. A drain is also provided on the fuel strainer (gascolator) located on the lower left side of the firewall, forward of the engine.

3. How often should you check for water, sediment, and fuel type/grade in the tanks? (AFM)

Both drains should be opened daily prior to the first flight.

F. Electrical

1. Describe the electrical system on your helicopter. (AFM)

The electrical system includes a 14-volt, 60-ampere alternator, voltage regulator or controller, battery contactor, and 12-volt, 25 ampere-hour batteries.

2. What is the function of an alternator? (AC 65-9A)

An electrical generator is a machine which converts mechanical energy into electrical energy by electromagnetic induction.

3. How do the magnetos work? (FAA-H-8083-25)

A magneto uses a permanent magnet to generate an electrical current completely independent of the aircraft's electrical system. The magneto generates sufficiently high voltage to jump a spark across the spark plug gap in each cylinder. The system begins to fire when you engage the starter and the crankshaft begins to turn. It continues to operate whenever the crankshaft is rotating.

4. How can you tell if a magneto is malfunctioning? (FAA-H-8083-25)

You can identify a malfunctioning ignition system during the pre-takeoff check by observing the decrease in RPM that occurs when you first move the ignition switch from BOTH to RIGHT, and then from BOTH to LEFT. A small decrease in engine RPM is normal during this check. The permissible decrease is listed in the AFM or POH. If the engine stops running when you switch to one magneto or if the RPM drop exceeds the allowable limit, do not fly the helicopter until the problem is corrected. The cause could be fouled plugs, broken or shorted wires between the magneto and the plugs, or improperly timed firing of the plugs. It should be noted that "no drop" in RPM is not normal, and in that instance, the helicopter should not be flown.

5. How many tachometers does your helicopter have? (AFM)

Two, one for the rotor RPM, and a second for the engine RPM.

6. When does the low rotor RPM light and horn come on? (AFM)

The low RPM light and horn indicate rotor RPM at 97% or below.

G. Flight Instruments

1. What are the required instruments for VFR flight? (14 CFR 91.205)

Manifold pressure gauge
Altimeter tach (rotor)
Shoulder harness
Fuel gauge
Oil temperature gauge
Oil pressure gauge
Magnetic compass airspeed
Indicator tachometer (engine)
Seatbelt

2. What are the required instruments for night VFR? (14 CFR 91.205 and AFM)

Instrument illumination lights (in POH)
Fuses — one spare set or three of each kind
Landing lights (for hire)
Anti-collision lights (red or white)
Position lights source of power

3. In addition to 14 CFR 91.205, what are the required instruments for the R-22 helicopter? (AFM)

Governor
Outside air temperature gauge
Alternator
Low RPM warning system

4. Is an emergency locator transmitter (ELT) required on helicopters? (14 CFR 91.207)

No, in §91.207 it states, "No person may operate a U.S.-registered civil *airplane* unless…" Because it says airplane, helicopters do not need to have an ELT installed for Part 91 operations.

H. Environmental

1. What does the cabin heat system consist of? (AFM)

The cabin heat system consists of an electric blower on the left side of the engine compartment, a heat shroud over the muffler, a control valve on the forward side of the firewall, an outlet grille forward of the pilots seat or tail rotor pedals, and the interconnecting ducts between components.

2. How does the cabin heat work?

Fresh air, heated by the exhaust shroud, is directed to the cabin, in front of the pilot's seat or tail rotor pedals, through a series of ducts.

I. Carburetor Heat

1. How does the carburetor heat system work? (FAA-H-8083-25)

Carburetor heat is an anti-icing system that preheats the air before it reaches the carburetor. Carburetor heat is intended to keep the fuel/air mixture above the freezing temperature to prevent the formation of carburetor ice. Carburetor heat can be used to melt ice that has already formed in the carburetor provided that the accumulation is not too great.

2. When should you use carburetor heat? (AFM)

- At power settings above 18 inches MAP, apply carburetor heat as required to keep CAT gauge needle out of the yellow arc.
- At power settings below 18 inches MAP, ignore gauge and apply full carburetor heat (CAT gauge does not indicate correct carburetor temperature below 18 inches MAP).

Emergency Operations

6

A. Power Failure at a Hover

1. Describe how to recover from a power failure below 8 feet AGL. (POH)

   a. Apply right pedal as required to prevent yawing.

   b. Allow aircraft to settle.

   c. Raise collective just before touchdown to cushion landing.

2. Describe how to recover from a power failure at a hover. (POH)

   a. Apply right pedal as required to prevent yawing.

   b. Allow aircraft to settle.

   c. Raise collective just before touchdown to cushion landing.

B. Power Failure at Altitude

1. Describe how to recover from a power failure at altitude. (POH)

   a. Lower collective immediately to maintain RPM and enter normal autorotation.

   b. Establish a steady glide at approximately 65 KIAS.

   c. Adjust collective to keep RPM in the green arc or apply full down collective if lightweight prevents attaining above 97% RPM.

   d. Select landing spot and, if altitude permits, maneuver so landing will be into the wind.

   e. A restart may be attempted at pilot's discretion if sufficient time is available.

Continued

f. If unable to restart, turn off unnecessary switches and shut off fuel.

g. At about 40 feet AGL, begin cyclic flare to reduce rate of descent and forward speed.

h. At about 8 feet AGL, apply forward cyclic to level ship and raise collective.

i. Just before touchdown, raise the collective to cushion landing.

j. Touchdown in a level attitude with nose straight ahead.

2. What is the maximum glide configuration for your helicopter when it is in autorotation? (POH)

a. Airspeed approximately 75 KIAS

b. Rotor RPM approximately 90%

c. Best glide ratio is about 4:1 or one nautical mile per 1,500 feet AGL

Note: Increase rotor RPM to 97% minimum when autorotation below 500 feet AGL.

C. Systems and Equipment Malfunctions

1. What procedures should be followed if an engine fire develops in flight? (POH)

a. Enter autorotation.

b. Master battery switch *OFF* (if time permits).

c. Cabin heat *OFF* (if installed and time permits).

d. Cabin vent *ON* (if time permits).

e. If engine is running, perform normal landing and immediately shut off fuel valve.

f. If engine stops running, shut off fuel valve and execute an autorotation landing.

2. What is the correct procedure if the tachometer fails in flight? (POH)

If rotor or engine tach malfunctions in flight, use remaining tach to monitor RPM. If it is not clear which tach is malfunctioning or if both tachometers are malfunctioning, allow governor to control RPM and land as soon as practical.

3. What is the correct procedure if the governor fails in flight? (POH)

If the engine RPM governor malfunctions, grip throttle firmly to override the governor, then switch governor off. Complete the flight using manual throttle control.

4. What action should be taken if a main rotor temperature, main rotor chip, or a tail rotor chip light was to illuminate during flight? (POH)

If light is accompanied by any indication of a problem such as noise, vibration, or temperature rise, land immediately. If there is no other indication of a problem, land as soon as practical.

5. What action should be taken if the clutch light illuminates in flight? (POH)

The clutch light may come on momentarily during run-up or during flight to re-tension the belts as they warm-up and stretch slightly. This is normal. If the light flickers or comes on in flight and does not go out within 8 seconds, pull the clutch circuit breaker, reduce power, and land immediately. Be prepared to enter autorotation.

D. Settling-With-Power

1. What is vortex ring state (settling with power)? (FAA-H-8083-21)

Vortex ring state describes an aerodynamic condition where a helicopter may be in a vertical descent with up to maximum power applied, and little or no cyclic authority. The term "settling with power" comes from the fact that the helicopter keeps settling even though full engine power is applied.

2. How is vortex ring state identified? (FAA-H-8083-21)

A fully developed vortex ring state is characterized by an unstable condition where the helicopter experiences uncommanded pitch and roll oscillations, has little or no cyclic authority, and achieves a descent rate, which, if allowed to develop, may approach 6,000 feet per minute. Increased levels of vibration accompany it.

3. During what maneuvers could the helicopter encounter a vortex ring state? (FAA-H-8083-21)

A vortex ring state may be encountered during any maneuver that places the main rotor in a condition of high up flow and low forward airspeed. This condition is sometimes seen during quick-stop type maneuvers or during recoveries from autorotations.

4. What is required for the development of vortex ring state? (FAA-H-8083-21)

The following combinations of conditions are likely to cause settling in a vortex ring state:

a. A vertical or nearly vertical descent of at least *300 feet per minute*. (Actual critical rate depends on the gross weight, RPM, density altitude, and other pertinent factors.)

b. The rotor system must be using some of the available engine power *(from 20 to 100 percent)*.

c. The horizontal velocity must be *slower than effective translational lift (ETL)*.

5. **What are the recovery procedures from vortex ring state?**

   Recovery is accomplished by increasing forward speed, and/or partially lowering collective pitch (if altitude permits). In a fully developed vortex ring state, the only recovery option may be to enter autorotation to break the vortex ring state. When cyclic authority is regained, forward airspeed can then be increased.

E. Low RPM Recovery

1. **What conditions are conducive to low RPM?**
   (FAA-H-8083-21)

   Under certain conditions of high weight, high temperature, or high-density altitude, you might get into a situation where the RPM is low even though you are using maximum throttle.

2. **What causes low RPM blade stall?** (FAA-H-8083-21)

   Low RPM stall is usually the result of the main rotor blades having an angle of attack that has created so much drag that engine power is not sufficient to maintain or attain normal operating RPM.

3. **How do you recover from low RPM?** (POH)

   To restore RPM, immediately and simultaneously roll throttle on, lower collective, if in forward flight, apply aft cyclic.

F. Anti-Torque System Failure

1. What is loss of tail rotor effectiveness (LTE)?
(FAA-H-8083-21)

It is the result of the tail rotor not providing adequate thrust to maintain directional control, and is usually caused by either certain wind directions while hovering, or by an insufficient tail rotor thrust for a given power setting at higher altitudes.

2. What should you do if you have a loss of tail rotor thrust during forward flight? (POH)

a. LTE is usually indicated by a nose right yaw, which cannot be corrected by applying left pedal.

b. Immediately enter autorotation.

c. Maintain at least 70 KIAS airspeed if practical.

d. Select a landing site, roll throttle into over-travel spring and perform autorotation landing.

Note: When a suitable landing site is not available, the vertical fin may permit limited controlled flight at very low power settings and airspeeds above 70 KIAS; however, prior to reducing airspeed, re-enter full autorotation.

3. What should you do if you have a loss of tail rotor thrust during a hover? (POH)

a. The failure is usually indicated by a nose right yaw, which cannot be stopped by applying left pedal.

b. Immediately roll throttle off into overtravel spring and allow aircraft to settle.

c. Raise collective just before touchdown to cushion landing.

G. Dynamic Rollover

1. What is a dynamic rollover? (FAA-H-8083-21)

Dynamic rollover is the tendency of a helicopter to continue rolling when the critical angle is exceeded. Dynamic rollover begins when the helicopter starts to pivot around its skid or wheel.

2. When does dynamic rollover occur? (FAA-H-8083-21)

Dynamic rollover can occur for a variety of reasons, including the failure to remove a tie down or skid securing device, or if the skid or wheel contacts a fixed object while hovering sideward, or if the gear is stuck in ice, soft asphalt, or mud. Dynamic rollover may also occur if you do not use the proper landing or takeoff technique or while performing slope operations.

3. What action should be taken by the pilot in a dynamic rollover situation? (FAA-H-8083-21)

Once started, dynamic rollover cannot be stopped by application of opposite cyclic control alone. For example, the right skid contacts an object and becomes the pivot point while the helicopter starts rolling to the right. Even with full left cyclic applied, the main rotor thrust vector and its moment follows the aircraft as it continues rolling to the right. Quickly lowering the collective is the most effective way to stop dynamic rollover from developing.

4. What is the critical angle in a dynamic rollover situation? (FAA-H-8083-21)

The critical angle is an angle of bank in a dynamic rollover, beyond which it is impossible to stop further roll, the helicopter will continue to roll onto its side.

H. Ground Resonance

1. What is ground resonance? (FAA-H-8083-21)

Ground resonance is an aerodynamic phenomenon associated with fully articulated rotor systems. It develops when the rotor blades move out of phase with each other and cause the rotor disc to become unbalanced. This condition can cause a helicopter to self-destruct in a matter of seconds.

However, for this condition to occur, the helicopter must be in contact with the ground. If you allow your helicopter to touch down firmly on one corner (wheel type landing gear is most conducive for this) the shock is transmitted to the main rotor system. This may cause the blades to move out of their normal relationship with each other. This movement occurs along the drag hinge.

2. How do you correct ground resonance? (FAA-H-8083-21)

If the RPM is in the normal operating range, you should fly the helicopter off the ground, and allow the blades to automatically realign themselves. You can then make a normal touchdown. If you lift off and allow the helicopter to firmly re-contact the surface before the blades are realigned, a second shock could move the blades again and aggravate the already unbalanced condition. This could lead to a violent, uncontrollable oscillation.

If the RPM is *low,* the corrective action to stop ground resonance is to close the throttle immediately and fully lower the collective to place the blades in low pitch.

If the RPM is in the *normal* operating range, you should fly the helicopter off the ground, and allow the blades to automatically realign themselves.

3. Does ground resonance occur in semi-rigid or rigid rotor systems? (FAA-H-8083-21)

This situation does not occur in rigid or semi-rigid rotor systems, because there is no drag hinge. In addition, skid type landing gear are not as prone to ground resonance as wheel type gear.

I. Low-G Conditions

1. Describe low-G conditions.

Pushing the cyclic control forward abruptly from either straight-and-level flight or after a climb can put the helicopter into a low-G (weightless) flight condition. In forward flight, when a push-over is performed, the angle of attack and thrust of the rotor is reduced, causing a low-G or weightless flight condition. During the low-G condition, the lateral cyclic has little, if any, effect because the rotor thrust has been reduced. Also, in a counter-clockwise rotor system (a clockwise system would be the reverse), there is no main rotor thrust component to the left to counteract the tail rotor thrust to the right, and since the tail rotor is above the CG, the tail rotor thrust causes the helicopter to roll rapidly to the right, If you attempt to stop the right roll by applying full left cyclic before re-gaining main rotor thrust, the rotor can exceed its flapping limits and cause structural failure of the rotor shaft due to mast bumping, or it may allow a blade to contact the airframe.

2. Why are low-G pushovers prohibited?

During a low-G pushover, the main rotor torque reaction will combine with tail rotor thrust to produce a powerful right rolling moment on the fuselage. With no lift from the rotor, there is no lateral control to stop the rapid right roll so mast bumping can occur. Severe inflight mast bumping usually results in main rotor shaft separation and/or rotor blade contact with the fuselage.

3. How can the pilot prevent low-G conditions?
(FAA-H-8083-21)

The best way to prevent a low-G situation from happening is to avoid the conditions where it might occur. This means avoiding turbulence as much as possible. If you do encounter turbulence, slow your forward airspeed and make small control inputs. If turbulence becomes excessive, consider making a precautionary landing. To help prevent turbulence-induced inputs; make sure your cyclic arm is properly supported. One way to accomplish this is to brace your arm against your leg. Even if you are not in turbulent conditions, you should avoid abrupt movement of the cyclic and collective.

4. What is the corrective action upon recognition of a low-G condition?

If you do find yourself in a low-G condition, which can be recognized by a feeling of weightlessness and an uncontrolled roll to the right, you should immediately and smoothly apply aft cyclic. Do not attempt to correct the rolling action with lateral cyclic. By applying aft cyclic, you will load the rotor system, which in turn produces thrust. Once thrust is restored, left cyclic control becomes effective, and you can roll the helicopter to a level attitude.

Helicopter Operations:
Instrument Rating

Instrument
Helicopter

1

1. An applicant for an instrument helicopter rating must have at least how much and what type of flight time as a pilot? (14 CFR 61.65)

An applicant must have:

A total of 40 hours of actual or simulated instrument time on the areas of operation of this section, to include—

- 15 hours of instrument flight training from an authorized instructor in the aircraft category for which the instrument rating is sought;

- 3 hours of instrument training that is appropriate to the instrument rating sought from an authorized instructor in preparation for the practical test within the 60 days preceding the date of the test.

2. What are the takeoff minimums for helicopters under 14 CFR Part 91,121,125,129, or 135? (14 CFR 91.175)

For Part 91, none. For Parts 121, 125, 129, 135: 1/2 statute mile visibility.

3. What are the fuel requirements for helicopters on an IFR flight? (14 CFR 91.167)

The helicopter must carry enough fuel to complete the flight to the first airport of intended landing, (including the approach), fly to an alternate (if needed), and fly after that for 30 minutes at normal cruising speed.

4. When are you required to file an alternate airport? (14 CFR 91.167)

For helicopters, an alternate is always required unless; weather reports or forecasts indicate that at the estimated time of arrival and for 1 hour afterwards, the ceiling will be at least 1,000 feet above the airport elevation, or at least 400 feet above the lowest approach minima, whichever is higher, and the visibility will be at least 2 statute miles.

5. What weather must be present at the airport to be able to file it as an alternate? (14 CFR 91.167)

Weather reports or forecasts must show ceilings at least 200 feet above the minimum for the approach to be flown, and visibility at least 1 statute mile but never less than the minimum visibility for the approach to be flown.

6. What approach categories do helicopter use when flying a SIAP?

Helicopters are category A aircraft. An aircraft only fits in one category. However, if it is necessary to operate at a speed in excess of the upper limit of the speed range for an aircraft's category, the minimums for that speed category shall be used.

7. Can helicopters flying conventional (non-copter) SIAPs reduce the visibility minima? (14 CFR 97.3)

Yes. "Helicopters may also use the Category A minimum descent altitude (MDA) or decision height (DH). The required visibility minimum may be reduced to one-half the published visibility minimum for category A aircraft, but in no case may it be reduced to less than one-quarter mile or 1,200 feet RVR."

8. What are the speed limits on GPS approaches and departures? (AIM 1-1-19)

Helicopter procedures should be flown at 70 knots or less since helicopter departure procedures and missed approaches use a 20:1 obstacle clearance surface (OCS), which is double the fixed wing OCS, and turning areas are based on this speed as well.

9. Is there a speed limit on conventional (non-copter) SIAPs? (AIM 10-1-2)

Helicopters may start an approach at speeds reaching the upper range of the approach category for the procedure. However airspeed must be slowed to 90 KIAS or less at the missed approach point (MAP) in order to apply the visibility reduction. Pilots are cautioned that such deceleration on an approach may make early identification of wind shear on the approach path difficult or impossible.

10. What are the speed limits on flying a GPS Copter SIAPs? (AIM 10-1-2)

Helicopters flying GPS Copter SIAPs must limit airspeed to 90 KIAS or less when flying any segment of the procedure, except speeds must be limited to no more than 70 KIAS on the final and missed approach segments. No reductions are allowed to the published minimums.

11. Can helicopters flying Copter SIAPs reduce the visibility minima? (AIM 10-1-2)

Helicopters flying Copter SIAPs may use the published minima, with no reductions allowed. The maximum airspeed is 90 KIAS on any segment of the approach or missed approach.

12. What are helicopter point-in-space approaches? (AIM 10-1-3)

Point-in-space are nonprecision approaches normally developed for heliports not meeting design standards for an IFR heliport or heliports not located within 2,600 feet of the MAP. A helicopter point-in-space approach can be developed from conventional NAVAIDs or area navigation systems (including GPS). These procedures involve a visual segment between the MAP and the landing area.

13. What is the normal distance allowed for a helicopter during a procedure turn? (AIM 5-4-9)

The procedure turn maneuver must be executed within the distance specified in the profile view. The normal distance allowed is 10 miles. But this may be reduced to a minimum of 5 miles where only Category A or helicopters are operated. It may be increased to as much as 15 miles to accommodate high performance aircraft.

14. What are some of the causes for a CDI needle to fluctuate in a helicopter? (AIM 1-1-3)

Certain helicopter rotor speeds can cause the VOR course deviation indicator to fluctuate as much as plus or minus six degrees. Slight changes to the RPM setting will normally smooth out this roughness. Pilots are urged to check for this modulation phenomenon prior to reporting a VOR station or aircraft equipment for unsatisfactory operation.

Helicopter Operations:
Commercial Pilot

Certificates and Documents

1

A. Privileges and Limitations

1. Under Part 91 can you transport people from point A to point B for compensation or hire in a helicopter, or would that fall under Part 135 operations? (14 CFR 119.1)

Helicopter flights can be conducted for compensation or hire within a 25 statute mile radius of the airport of takeoff if—

- Not more than two passengers are carried in the helicopter in addition to the required flight crew;
- Each flight is made under day VFR conditions;
- The helicopter used is certificated in the standard category and complies with the 100-hour inspection requirements of Part 91;
- The operator notifies the FAA Flight Standards District Office responsible for the geographic area concerned at least 72 hours before each flight and furnishes any essential information that the office requests;
- The number of flights does not exceed a total of six in any calendar year;
- Each flight has been approved by the Administrator; and
- Cargo is not carried in or on the helicopter.

2. Can a commercial pilot carry passengers for hire in restricted, limited, or experimental category aircraft? (14 CFR 91.313)

No person may operate a restricted, a limited or an experimental category civil aircraft carrying persons or property for compensation or hire.

3. What are the requirements for the pilot to obtain a certificate under Part 133? (14 CFR 133.21–133.23)

a. The applicant must hold, or have available the services of at least one person who holds, a current commercial or ATP certificate, with a rating appropriate for the rotorcraft prescribed in §133.19.

b. The applicant must designate one pilot, who may be the applicant, as chief pilot for rotorcraft external-load operations. The applicant also may designate qualified pilots as assistant chief pilots to perform the functions of the chief pilot when the chief pilot is not readily available. The chief pilot and assistant chief pilots must be acceptable to the FAA and each must hold a current Commercial or ATP Certificate, with a rating appropriate for the rotorcraft prescribed in §133.19.

The applicant must also meet the requirements of §133.23 where by oral examination and test of skill the applicant will display and understanding of external load operations, and the ability to perform such operations.

4. How long is the external load certificate valid? (14 CFR 133.13)

Unless sooner surrendered, suspended, or revoked, a Rotorcraft External-Load Operator Certificate expires at the end of the twenty-fourth month after the month in which it is issued or renewed.

5. Can you operate a helicopter for compensation or hire inside of the Height Velocity diagram? (14 CFR Part 91)

Under Part 91 operations, flight within the H/V diagram is *not* prohibited. Pilots are encouraged to "avoid" the shaded area whenever possible.

B. Aircraft Certificates and Documents

1. What documents are required to be on board prior to flight? (14 CFR 91.9 and 91.203)

A irworthiness Certificate
R egistration Certificate
O perating Limitations
W eight and Balance Data

2. Are helicopter flight manuals required to be on board all aircraft? (14 CFR 91.9)

"No person may operate a civil aircraft without complying with the operating limitations specified in the approved Airplane or Rotorcraft Flight Manual, markings, and placards, or as otherwise prescribed by the certificating authority of the country of registry." In order to "operate" in compliance with the RFM, an RFM must be on board the helicopter.

3. What is the maximum operating density altitude for the R-22? (AFM)

Maximum operating density altitude is 14,000 feet.

Cross-Country Flight Planning

2

1. **Is flight within the flight velocity envelope prohibited to and from a heliport over water?** (14 CFR 91.9)

   Anyone flying a helicopter that is taking off or landing at a heliport built over water may fly momentarily through the prohibited range of the limiting height–speed envelope, provided the helicopter is amphibious, has floats or floatation gear and in any case can be ditched safely in open water.

2. **What are the instructions for helicopter operations at controlled airports?** (AIM 4-3-17)

   Whenever possible, helicopter operations will be instructed to avoid the flow of fixed-wing aircraft to minimize overall delays.

3. **Are there any exceptions to avoiding the flow of fixed-wing aircraft at a controlled airport?** (AIM 4-3-17)

   Yes. Because helicopter pilots are intimately familiar with the effects of rotor downwash, they are best qualified to determine if a given operation can be conducted safely. Some other exceptions would be IFR flights, avoidance of noise sensitive areas, or use of runways/taxiways to minimize rotor downwash.

4. **In what situation would a hover taxi be necessary?** (AIM 4-3-17)

   Taxi—used when it is intended or expected that the helicopter will taxi on the airport surface, either via taxiways or other prescribed routes. *Taxi* is used primarily for helicopters equipped with wheels or in response to a pilot request.

   Hover taxi—used when slow forward movement is desired or when it may be appropriate to move very short distances. Pilots should avoid this procedure if rotor downwash is likely to cause

   Continued

damage to parked aircraft or if blowing dust or snow could obscure visibility.

Air taxi—preferred method for helicopter ground movements on airports provided ground operations and conditions permit. Unless otherwise requested or instructed, pilots are expected to remain below 100 feet AGL.

At all times, helicopters should avoid over-flight of other aircraft, vehicles, and personnel during air-taxi operations.

5. **Are helicopters limited to the area from which they can take off or land?** (AIM 4-3-17)

Operations from nonmovement areas are conducted at pilot discretion and should be based on local policies, procedures, or letters of agreement. Helicopter operations may be conducted from a runway, taxiway, portion of a landing strip, or any clear area which could be used as a landing site such as the scene of an accident, a construction site, or the roof of a building. These areas may be improved or unimproved and may be separate from or located on an airport/heliport.

6. **Why is it important for helicopter pilots to always be mindful of the wind?** (AIM 4-3-17)

A pilot request to takeoff in a given direction indicates that the pilot is willing to accept the wind condition and controllers will honor the request if traffic permits. Departure points could be a significant distance from the control tower and it may be difficult or impossible for the controller to determine the helicopter's relative position to the wind.

7. **What is the difference in terminology when departing a movement vs. nonmovement area?** (AIM 4-3-17)

   Movement—"CLEARED FOR TAKEOFF FROM": (taxiway, helipad, runway number, etc.)

   Nonmovement—"PROCEED AS REQUESTED"

   When other known traffic is not a factor and takeoff is requested from an area not visible from the tower, an area not authorized for helicopter use, an unlighted area at night, or an area not on the airport, the phraseology "DEPARTURE FROM (location) WILL BE AT YOUR OWN RISK."

8. **What are the colors of the landing areas for helicopters?** (AIM 2-3-2)

   Markings defining the landing area on a heliport are white except for hospital heliports, which use a red "H" on a white cross.

Helicopter Landing Areas

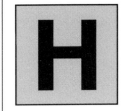
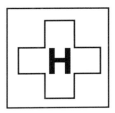

| Recommended Marking for Civil Heliports | Recommended Marking for Hospital Heliports | Recommended Marking for Closed Heliports |

9. **What is the "H" aligned with on a helipad?** (AIM 2-3-2)

   The letter "H" in the markings is oriented to align with the intended direction of approach.

10. **What is the specific frequency that the FCC has designated for air-to-air general aviation helicopters?** (AIM 4-1-11)

    123.025

11. What are the communication procedures with a control tower when the transmitter is inoperative? (AIM 4-2-13)

To acknowledge tower transmissions during daylight hours, hovering helicopters will turn in the direction of the controlling facility and flash the landing light. While in flight, helicopters should show their acknowledgement of receiving a transmission by making shallow banks in opposite directions. At night, helicopters will acknowledge receipt of transmissions by flashing either the landing or the searchlight.

12. What considerations regarding changing radio frequencies do controllers give to helicopter pilots in a hover? (AIM 4-3-14)

Controllers will normally avoid issuing a radio frequency change to helicopters known to be single-piloted which are hovering, air taxiing, or flying near the ground. At times, it may be necessary for pilots to alert ATC regarding single-pilot operations to minimize delay of essential ATC communications.

Performance and Limitations

3

A. Adverse Effects of Exceeding Limitations

1. Over what types of surfaces will ground effect be the most pronounced? (FAA-H-8083-21)

Ground effect is at its maximum in a no-wind condition over a firm, smooth surface. Tall grass, rough terrain, revetments, and water surfaces alter the airflow pattern, causing an increase in rotor tip vortices.

2. What is a major factor in determining V_{NE}? (FAA-H-8083-21)

Retreating blade stall is a major factor in limiting a helicopter's top forward speed (V_{NE}) and can be felt developing by a low frequency vibration, pitching up of the nose, and a roll in the direction of the retreating blade. However, an external load may further limit some helicopters' V_{NE}.

3. What is the correct procedure if you encounter severe turbulence in an R-22? (AFM)

Adjust forward airspeed to between 60 KIAS and 0.7 V_{NE} but no lower than 57 KIAS, upon inadvertently encountering moderate, severe, or extreme turbulence. Continued flight in moderate, severe, or extreme turbulence is prohibited.

4. Why does an out of ground effect (OGE) hover require more power than an in ground effect (IGE) hover in the same conditions? (FAA-H-8083-21)

In an OGE hover, airflow around the blade tips is no longer restricted, and the blade tip vortices increase with the decrease in outward airflow. As a result, induced drag increases, which means a higher pitch angle, and more power is needed to move the air down through the rotor.

5. **What is the danger if you exceed manifold pressure limits?** (AFM; FAA-H-8032-25)

For any given RPM, there is a manifold pressure that should not be exceeded. If manifold pressure is excessive for a given RPM, the pressure within the cylinders could be exceeded, thus placing undue stress on the cylinders. If repeated too frequently, this stress could weaken the cylinder components, and eventually cause engine failure. Exceeding manifold pressure limits could also result in demanding more power out of the engine than it is able to produce, first a decrease in rotor RPM will be apparent. If the condition is allowed to further increase, rotor stall is likely. Main rotor blade and/or a drive system failure could occur if the helicopter is repeatedly flown above its approved manifold pressure limit.

6. **What is the difference between limit manifold pressure and maximum continuous power?** (AFM)

LMP—Limit manifold pressure otherwise known as 5 minute takeoff rating. After 5 minutes, the collective should be lowered to maximum continuous power and all pertinent engine gauges checked for abnormalities.

MCP—Maximum continuous power is the maximum power to be used for any continuous period.

B. Height/Velocity Diagram

1. **Why is the H/V diagram used only for the takeoff profile, and not for the landing profile?** (FAA-H-8083-21)

An engine failure accruing in the upper section of the H/V diagram is most critical in a climb after takeoff. During a climb, a helicopter is operating at higher power settings and blade angle of attack. If descending when in the upper section of the diagram then an engine failure is less critical provided a safe landing area is available.

C. Loss of Tail Rotor Effectiveness

1. What are the three different types of LTE?
(FAA-H-8083-21)

Assuming a counterclockwise rotor system:

Main rotor disc interference—Winds at velocities of 10 to 30 knots from the left front cause the main rotor vortex to be blown into the tail rotor by the relative wind. The effect of this main rotor disc vortex causes the tail rotor to operate in an extremely turbulent environment.

Weathercock stability —When winds are coming from the rear of the helicopter, the helicopter attempts to weathervane its nose into the relative wind. Unless a resisting pedal input is made, the helicopter starts a slow, uncommanded turn to either the right or left depending upon the wind direction. If the pilot allows a yaw rate to develop, the yaw rate can accelerate rapidly.

Tail rotor vortex ring state—Winds coming from the left of the helicopter cause a tail rotor vortex ring state to develop. The result is a non-uniform, unsteady flow into the tail rotor. The vortex ring state causes tail rotor thrust variations, which result in yaw deviations. The net effect of the unsteady flow is an oscillation of tail rotor thrust. Rapid and continuous pedal movements are necessary to compensate for the rapid changes in tail rotor thrust when hovering in a crosswind. Maintaining a precise heading in this region is difficult, but this characteristic presents no significant problem unless corrective action is delayed.

D. Operating Limitations

1. Why are airplane pilots considered "high risk" when flying helicopters? (AFM)

An experienced airplane pilot's ingrained reactions can be deadly when flying a helicopter. The airplane pilot, when required to react suddenly or under unexpected circumstances, may revert to airplane reactions and commit a fatal error. Under those conditions, his or her hands and feet move purely by reaction without conscious thought.

2. **When is translating tendency most significant?** (FAA-H-8083-21)

The translating tendency is most significant in a hover when the tail rotor thrust need is the greatest.

3. **What are some of the indications of retreating blade stall?** (FAA-H-8083-21)

Retreating blade stall can be felt developing by a low frequency vibration, pitching up of the nose, and a roll in the direction of the retreating blade.

4. **What is the recovery procedure from retreating blade stall?** (FAA-H-8083-21)

Correct recovery from retreating blade stall requires the collective to be lowered first, which reduces blade angles and thus angle of attack. Aft cyclic can then be used to slow the helicopter.

Aircraft
Performance Charts **4**

The following are typical helicopter performance questions.
Refer to your aircraft's POH for correct answers.

1. **What is the IGE hover height for an R-22 Beta helicopter on a +10°C day with 1,350 pounds? (AFM)**

   Approximately 7,000 foot pressure altitude.

2. **What is the OGE hover height for R-22 Beta II helicopter on a -10°C day with 1,370 pounds? (AFM)**

   Approximately 6,000 foot pressure altitude.

3. **What would be the MCP and LMP for a Beta at +20°C OAT and 5,500 foot pressure altitude? (AFM)**

   MCP 22.8

   LMP 22.5

4. **What is the V_{NE} for a Beta at 5,500-foot pressure altitude and +20°C? (AFM)**

   Approximately 90 KIAS.

5. **What is the V_{NE} for a Beta at 6,000-foot pressure altitude and +30°C? (AFM)**

   Approximately 87 KIAS.

6. **What is the V_{NE} for a Beta II at 6,000-foot pressure altitude and +15°C? (AFM)**

   88.5 KIAS

7. **What is the V_{NE} for a Beta II at 7,000-foot pressure altitude and +10°C? (AFM)**

   85 KIAS

Helicopter Systems

5

A. Primary Flight Controls

1. What type of trim system is installed on the helicopter? (AFM)

The lateral cyclic is equipped with an on/off trim spring to cancel the left stick force, which occurs during high-speed flight. A push-pull knob actuates the spring.

2. What system keeps the collective from lowering in flight? (AFM)

The friction system, which consists of a toggle type lever, is located near the aft end of the center collective stick. It is actuated aft to increase friction and forward to release it.

3. Does the helicopter have cyclic friction? (AFM)

Yes, the cyclic friction knob is located to the left of the cyclic stick. Turning the knob clockwise applies friction to both longitudinal and lateral cyclic. Cyclic friction is normally applied only on the ground. It is not recommended to apply cyclic friction in flight.

4. What are trim tabs?

Trim tabs are located on the trailing edge of the main rotor blades. They are used to adjust each individual main rotor blade, in its plane of rotation, for track-and-balance purposes.

5. What is the danger of lowering the collective too quickly during powered flight above 4,000 feet? (AFM)

At high power settings above 4,000 feet, an overspeed may occur if the throttle is not reduced when collective is lowered quickly.

6. Are there any concerns for flying near broadcast towers? (AFM)

Electrical system malfunctions have occurred in aircraft flying near high intensity broadcast towers. Under these conditions the governor may react erratically and could overspeed the engine and rotor.

B. Powerplant

1. How is the engine cooled? (AFM)

A direct-drive, squirrel-cage cooling fan mounted to the engine output shaft supplies cooling air to the cylinders and oil cooler via a fiberglass and aluminum shroud. Ducts from the shroud supply cooling air to the alternator and main rotor gearbox.

2. How does the carburetor heat system work on the R-22? (AFM)

A hot air scoop supplies heated air to the air box. A sliding valve controlled by the pilot allows either cool or warm air to flow into the box, through the air filter, and up into the carburetor.

3. How does carburetor affect the helicopter? (FAA-H-8083-21)

Carburetor heat is intended to keep the fuel/air mixture above the freezing temperature to prevent the formation of carburetor ice. Carburetor heat can be used to melt ice that has already formed in the carburetor if the accumulation is not too great.

4. How can a failure of a drive system bearing be detected? (AFM)

The pilot should open his right door, uncover his right ear, and listen to the sound of the drive system both during start-up and during shutdown.

5. **What are the airspeed color code markings for the R-22? (AFM)**

Green arc .... 50 to 102 KIAS
Red line .... 102 KIAS

6. **What are the oil pressure limitations? (AFM)**

Minimum during idle .... 25 psi
Minimum during flight .... 55 psi
Maximum during flight .... 95 psi
Maximum during start
and warm-up .... 115 psi
Minimum .... 90% (459 RPM)

7. **Why is there a lower yellow arc on the tachometers? (AFM)**

Due to tail rotor drive shaft resonance, the pilot is asked to avoid continuous operation in the yellow arc.

8. **What are the basic parts of a turbine engine?**

Compressor—A fan assembly consisting of a number of blades fixed on a rotating spindle. As the rotor turns, air is drawn rearwards. Stator vanes are arranged in fixed rows between the rotor blades and act as a diffuser at each stage to decrease air velocity and increase air pressure (compression effect). There may be a number of rows of rotor blades and stator vanes. Each row constitutes a pressure stage, and the number of stages depends on the amount of air and pressure rise required for the particular engine.

Combustion chamber—Unlike a piston engine, the combustion in a turbine engine is continuous. An igniter plug serves only to ignite the fuel/air mixture when starting the engine. Once the fuel/air mixture is ignited, it will continue to burn as long as the fuel/air mixture is present. If there is an interruption of fuel, air, or both, combustion ceases. This is known as a "flame-out," and the engine has to be restarted or relit. Some helicopters are equipped with auto-relight, which automatically activates the igniters to start combustion if the engine flames out.

Continued

Turbine—The turbine section consists of a series of turbine wheels that are used to drive the compressor section and the rotor system. The first stage, which is usually referred to as the gas producer or N_1 may consist of one or more turbine wheels. This stage drives the components necessary to complete the turbine cycle making the engine self-sustaining. Common components driven by the N_1 stage are the compressor, oil pump, and fuel pump. The second stage, which may also consist of one or more wheels, is dedicated to driving the main rotor system and accessories from the engine gearbox. This is referred to as the power turbine (N_2 or N_R).

If the first and second stage turbines are mechanically coupled to each other, the system is said to be a direct-drive engine or fixed turbine. These engines share a common shaft, which means the first and second stage turbines, and thus the compressor and output shaft, are connected.

On most turbine assemblies used in helicopters, the first stage and second stage turbines are not mechanically connected to each other. Rather, they are mounted on independent shafts and can turn freely with respect to each other. This is referred to as a "free turbine." When the engine is running, the combustion gases pass through the first stage turbine to drive the compressor rotor, and then past the independent second stage turbine, which turns the gearbox to drive the output shaft.

C. Main Rotor and Anti-Torque Rotor

1. What is the actual RPM of the rotor when the tachometer indicates 104%? (AFM)

530 RPM

2. What are the "power on" maximum and minimum rotor RPM for the R-22? (AFM)

Maximum .... 104% (530 RPM)
Minimum .... O-360 engine: 101% (515 RPM)
Minimum .... O-320 engine: 97% (495 RPM)

3. What are the "power off" maximum and minimum rotor RPM for the R-22? (AFM)

Maximum .... 110% (561 RPM)

Minimum .... 90% (459 RPM)

4. When would you use a symmetrical airfoil over an asymmetrical airfoil? (FAA-H-8083-21)

Symmetrical blades are very stable, which helps keep blade twisting and flight control loads to a minimum. This stability is achieved by keeping the center of pressure virtually unchanged as the angle of attack changes. One of the reasons an asymmetrical rotor blade is not as stable as a symmetrical rotor blade, is that the center of pressure changes with changes in angle of attack. Main rotor blades are usually symmetrical where tail rotor blades are usually asymmetrical.

5. Other than the variable pitch tail rotor, what are some examples of the different types of anti-torque systems? (FAA-H-8083-21)

Fenstrom—This system uses a series of rotating blades shrouded within a vertical tail. Because the blades are located within a circular duct, they are less likely to be exposed to people or objects.

NOTAR ("no tail rotor")—The NOTAR system is an alternative to the anti-torque rotor. The system forces low-pressure air into the tail boom by a fan mounted within the helicopter. The air is then fed through horizontal slots, located on the right side of the tail boom, and to a controllable rotating nozzle to provide anti-torque and directional control.

6. Why are some rotor systems under-slung? (FAA-H-8083-21)

To decrease the change in distance of the center of mass from the axis of rotation when compensating for Coriolis effect. If they were not under-slung the hunting action would be absorbed by the blades through bending.

7. **How does a fully articulated rotor system compensate for Coriolis effect?** (FAA-H-8083-21)

A series of hinges allow the blades to move independently of one another. The back and forth movement of the blades is controlled by drag hinges and dampers and these compensate for the acceleration and deceleration caused by Coriolis effect.

D. Helicopter Skids, Brakes, Steering, or Frame

1. **How is the tail cone structured?** (AFM)

The tail cone is a monocoque structure in which the aluminum skins carry the primary loads.

2. **Can items be attached to the skids?** (AFM)

The landing gear is optimized to take high "up" loads. Consequently, it has very low strength in the opposite or "down" direction. Even a small weight attached to the landing gear may change the natural frequency enough to cause high loads due to inflight vibration.

3. **What are the different types of external loads?**
(14 CFR Part 133 and ASA-PHF)

Class A rotorcraft and load combination means one in which the external load cannot move freely, cannot be jettisoned, and does not extend below landing the gear.

Class B rotorcraft and load combinations means one in which the external load is jettison-able and is lifted free of land or water during the rotorcraft operation.

Class C rotorcraft and load combination means one in which the external load is jettison-able and remains in contact with land or water during the rotorcraft operations.

Class D rotorcraft and load combination means one in which the external load is other than a class A, B, or C, and has been specifically approved by the FAA for that operation.

E. Electrical

1. What do each one of the warning lights indicates? (AFM)

Oil—Indicates loss of engine power or oil pressure

AIR Temp—Indicates excessive temperature of main rotor gearbox

MR Chip—Indicates metallic particles in main rotor gearbox

TR Chip—Indicates metallic particles in tail rotor gearbox

Low Fuel—Indicates approximately one gallon of usable fuel remaining

Clutch—Indicates that the clutch actuator circuit is on, either engaging or disengaging the clutch

AL—Indicates low voltage and possible alternator failure

Brake—Indicates rotor brake is engaged

Starter "On"—Indicates starter motor is engaged

Gov Off—Indicates engine RPM throttle governor is off

Low RPM—A horn and an illuminated caution light indicate that rotor RPM may be below safe limits

F. Avionics Equipment

1. How do the tachometers work? (AFM)

Breaker points in the right magneto provide the signal for the engine tachometer. The sensor for the *rotor* tachometer senses the passage of two magnets attached to the main gearbox drive yoke.

2. From where do the tachometers receive their power? (AFM)

Each tachometer circuit has a separate circuit breaker and is completely independent from the other. The tachometers can receive power from the alternator or the battery. With the MASTER BATTERY switch off, the tachometer bus continues to receive power as long as the clutch switch is in the engage position.

3. How does a radar altimeter work?

A radar altimeter on board the helicopter transmits signals at high frequency (over 1,700 pulses per second) and receives the echo from the surface. This is analyzed to derive a precise measurement of the round-trip time between the instrument and the surface. The time measurement, scaled by the speed of light (at which electro-magnetic waves travel), yields a range measurement. By averaging the estimates over a second, this produces a very accurate measurement of range. However, as electromagnetic waves travel through the atmosphere, they can be decelerated by water vapor or by ionization.

Emergency Procedures

6

A. Power Failure at Altitude

1. Why is it good to practice autorotations within glide distance of a smooth open area? (POH)

There have been instances when the engine has quit during simulated engine failures. As a precaution, always perform the simulated engine failure within glide distance of a smooth open area where you are certain you could complete a safe touchdown autorotation should it become necessary. Also, wait until you have been flying for at least 15 to 20 minutes.

2. With respect to power failure at altitude, how can the pilot manipulate the autorotation to shorten or lengthen the glide?

To shorten the glide of an autorotation, the pilot must lower the airspeed and increase the rotor RPMs. This will increase the approach angle and increase rate of descent.

To lengthen the glide of the autorotation the pilot must increase the airspeed and lower rotor RPMs. This will shallow out the approach angle and decrease the rate of descent.

For maximum glide distance configuration, see RFM.

3. What are the procedures for a 180° autorotation with a turn? (FAA-H-8083-21)

Changes in the aircraft's attitude and the angle of bank cause a corresponding change in rotor RPM. Adjust the collective as necessary in the turn to maintain rotor RPM in the green arc. At the 90° point, check the progress of your turn by glancing toward your landing area. Plan the second 90 degrees of turn to roll out on the centerline. If you are too close, decrease the bank angle; if too far

Continued

out, increase the bank angle. Keep the helicopter in trim with anti-torque pedals. The turn should be completed and the helicopter aligned with the intended touchdown area prior to passing through 100 feet AGL.

B. Low Rotor RPM

1. Can a helicopter recover from blade stall? (FAA-H-8083-21)

No. If you let rotor RPM decay to the point where all the rotor blades stall, the result is usually fatal, especially when it occurs at altitude. The danger of low rotor RPM and blade stall is greatest in small helicopters with low blade inertia.

C. Dynamic Rollover

1. What can be done by the pilot to reduce the risk of dynamic rollover? (FAA-H-8083-21)

a. The collective should not be pulled suddenly to get airborne, as a large and abrupt rolling moment in the opposite direction could occur. Pull in just enough collective pitch control to be light on the skids and feel for equilibrium, then gently lift the helicopter into the air.

b. Always practice hovering autorotations into the wind, but never when the wind is gusty or over 10 knots.

c. When hovering close to fences, sprinklers, bushes, runway/taxi lights, or other obstacles that could catch a skid, use extreme caution.

d. When practicing hovering maneuvers close to the ground, make sure you hover high enough to have adequate skid clearance with any obstacles, especially when practicing sideways or rearward flight.

e. If passengers or cargo are loaded or unloaded, the lateral cyclic requirement changes.

f. Do not allow the cyclic limits to be reached. If the cyclic control limit is reached, further lowering of the collective may cause mast bumping. If this occurs, return to a hover and select a landing point with a lesser degree of slope.

g. During a takeoff from a slope, if the upslope skid/wheel starts to leave the ground before the downslope skid/wheel, smoothly and gently lower the collective and check to see if the downslope skid/wheel is caught on something. Under these conditions, vertical ascent is the only acceptable method of liftoff.

h. During flight operations on a floating platform, if the platform is pitching/rolling while attempting to land or takeoff, the result could be dynamic rollover.

2. **What situations are most critical for a helicopter with counterclockwise main rotor rotation to be in danger of dynamic rollover?** (FAA-H-8083-21)

- Right side skid/wheel down, since translating tendency adds to the rollover force.
- Right lateral center of gravity.
- Crosswinds from the left.
- Left yaw inputs.

For helicopters with clockwise rotor rotation, the opposite would be true.

3. **When landing on a slope, can the helicopter reach critical angle and roll uphill?**

Yes. If too much cyclic is held into the slope when the downslope skid has been raised, the aircraft may roll uphill.

D. Retreating Blade Stall

1. What conditions aggravate retreating blade stall? (FAA-H-8083-21)

High weight, low rotor RPM, high density altitude, turbulence and/or steep abrupt turns are all conducive to retreating blade stall at high forward airspeeds. As altitude is increased, higher blade angles are required to maintain lift at a given airspeed. Thus, retreating blade stall is encountered at a lower forward airspeed at altitude.

2. What are some of the other reasons for limiting V_{NE}?

High gross weight—as it increases, V_{NE} will be reduced

Increasing density altitude will decrease V_{NE}

External loads will reduce V_{NE}

Door-off operations will also reduce V_{NE} in some aircraft

Helicopter Operations:
Certified Flight Instructor

Principles of Flight

1

A. Characteristics of Different Rotor Systems

1. How is each blade attached to the fully articulated rotor hub? (FAA-H-8083-21)

Each rotor blade is attached to the rotor hub by a horizontal hinge, called the flapping hinge, which permits the blades to flap up and down. Each blade can move up and down independently of the others. The flapping hinge may be located at varying distances from the rotor hub, and there may be more than one.

2. How is feathering accomplished in the semi-rigid rotor system? (FAA-H-8083-21)

Feathering is accomplished by the feathering hinge, which changes the pitch angle of the blade.

B. Effect of Lift, Weight, Thrust, and Drag

1. What are the four dynamic forces that act on a helicopter during all maneuvers? (FAA-H-8083-21)

Lift—The upward acting force.

Gravity or Weight—The downward acting force.

Thrust—The forward acting force.

Drag—The backward acting force.

2. Explain the following terms as they relate to the production of lift. (FAA-H-8083-21)

Bernoulli's principle—As air velocity increases through the constricted portion of a venturi tube, the pressure decreases. Compare the upper surface of an airfoil with the constriction in a venturi tube that is narrower in the middle than at the ends. The upper half of the venturi tube can be replaced by layers of undisturbed air. Thus, as air flows over the upper surface of an airfoil, the camber of the airfoil causes an increase in the speed of the airflow. The increased speed of airflow results in a decrease in pressure on the upper surface of the airfoil. At the same time, air flows along the lower surface of the airfoil, building up pressure. The combination of decreased pressure on the upper surface and increased pressure on the lower surface results in an upward force.

Newton's Third Law—Additional lift is provided by the rotor blade's lower surface as air striking the underside is deflected downward. According to Newton's Third Law of Motion, "for every action there is an equal and opposite reaction," the air that is deflected downward also produces an upward (lifting) reaction.

3. Define the following terms. (FAA-H-8083-21)

Advancing blade—The blade moving in the same direction as the helicopter or gyroplane. In rotorcraft that have counterclockwise main rotor blade rotation as viewed from above, the advancing blade is in the right half of the rotor disc area during forward movement.

Airfoil—Any surface designed to obtain a useful action of lift, or negative lift, as it moves through the air.

Aircraft pitch—When referenced to an aircraft, it is the movement about its lateral, or pitch axis. Movement of the cyclic forward or aft causes the nose of the helicopter or gyroplane to pitch up or down.

Aircraft roll—The movement of the aircraft about its longitudinal axis. Movement of the cyclic right or left causes the helicopter or gyroplane to tilt in that direction.

Angle of attack—The angle between the airfoil's chord line and the relative wind.

Autorotation—The condition of flight during which the main rotor is driven only by aerodynamic forces with no power from the engine.

Blade feathering—The rotation of the blade around the span-wise (pitch change) axis.

Blade flap—The ability of the rotor blade to move in a vertical direction. Blades may flap independently or in unison.

Blade lead and lag—The fore and aft movement of the blade in the plane of rotation. It is sometimes called hunting or dragging.

Blade loading—The load imposed on rotor blades, determined by dividing the total weight of the helicopter by the combined area of all the rotor blades.

Blade root—The part of the blade that attaches to the blade grip.

Blade span—The length of a blade from its tip to its root.

Blade stall—The condition of the rotor blade when it is operating at an angle of attack greater than the maximum angle of lift.

Blade tip—The further most part of the blade from the hub of the rotor.

Blade track—The relationship of the blade tips in the plane of rotation. Blades that are in track will move through the same plane of rotation.

Blade twist—The variation in the angle of incidence of a blade between the root and the tip.

Blowback—The tendency of the rotor disc to tilt aft in forward flight as a result of flapping.

Centrifugal force—The apparent force that an object moving along a circular path exerts on the body constraining the object and that acts outwardly away from the center of rotation.

Centripetal force—The force that attracts a body toward its axis of rotation. It is opposite centrifugal force.

Chord line—An imaginary straight line between the leading and trailing edges of an airfoil section.

Chordwise axis—A term used in reference to semi-rigid rotors describing the flapping or teetering axis of the rotor.

Cyclic feathering—The mechanical change of the angle of incidence, or pitch, of individual rotor blades independently of other blades in the system.

Continued

Delta hinge—A flapping hinge with a skewed axis so that the flapping motion introduces a component of feathering that would result in a restoring force in the flap-wise direction.

Disc area—The area swept by the blades of the rotor. It is a circle with its center at the hub and has a radius of one blade length.

Disc loading—The total helicopter weight divided by the rotor disc area.

Flapping hinge—The hinge that permits the rotor blade to flap and thus balance the lift generated by the advancing and retreating blades.

Hunting—Movement of a blade with respect to the other blades in the plane of rotation, sometimes called leading or lagging.

Inertia—The property of matter by which it will remain at rest or in a state of uniform motion in the same direction unless acted upon by some external force.

Induced drag—That part of the total drag that is created by the production of lift.

Induced flow—The component of air flowing vertically through the rotor system resulting from the production of lift.

L/D$_{MAX}$—The maximum ratio between total lift (L) and total drag (D). This point provides the best glide speed. Any deviation from the best glide speed increases drag and reduces the distance you can glide.

Load factor—The ratio of a specified load to the total weight of the aircraft.

Parasite drag—The part of total drag created by the form or shape of helicopter parts.

Pendular action—The lateral or longitudinal oscillation of the fuselage due to it being suspended from the rotor system.

Pitch angle—The angle between the chord line of the rotor blade and the reference plane of the main rotor hub or the rotor plane of rotation.

Profile drag—Drag incurred from frictional or parasitic resistance of the blades passing through the air. It does not change significantly with the angle of attack of the airfoil section, but it increases moderately as airspeed increases.

Resultant relative wind—Airflow from rotation that is modified by induced flow.

Retreating blade—Any blade, located in a semicircular part of the rotor disc, where the blade direction is opposite to the direction of flight.

Solidity ratio—The ratio of the total rotor blade area to total rotor disc area.

Span—The dimension of a rotor blade or airfoil from root to tip.

Symmetrical rotor—An airfoil having the same shape on the top and bottom.

Teetering hinge—A hinge that permits the rotor blades of a semi-rigid rotor system to flap as a unit.

Unloaded rotor—The state of a rotor when rotor force has been removed, or when the rotor is operating under a low or negative G condition.

C. Torque Effect

1. Explain how torque effect plays into the design of a helicopter. (FAA-H-8083-21)

The main purpose of the tail rotor is to counteract the torque effect of the main rotor. Since torque varies with changes in power, the tail rotor thrust must also be varied.

2. How do the pedals compensate for torque effect? (FAA-H-8083-21)

The pedals are connected to the pitch change mechanism on the tail rotor gearbox and allow the pitch angle on the tail rotor blades to be increased or decreased.

3. How does a two-bladed rotor system compensate for torque effect? (FAA-H-8083-21)

On a two-bladed rotor system, each rotor will spin in opposite directions, thus canceling out each main rotor's torque effect.

D. Dissymmetry of Lift

1. How is dissymmetry of lift compensated for in a fully articulated rotor system? (FAA-H-8083-21)

In a fully articulated rotor system, the main rotor blades flap and feather automatically to equalize lift across the rotor disc. Articulated rotor systems, usually with three or more blades, incorporate a horizontal hinge (flapping hinge) to allow the individual rotor blades to move, or flap up and down as they rotate.

2. How is dissymmetry of lift compensated for in a semi-rigid rotor system? (FAA-H-8083-21)

A semi-rigid rotor system (two blades) uses a teetering hinge, which allows the blades to flap as a unit. When one blade flaps up, the other flaps down.

3. How is dissymmetry of lift compensated for in a fully rigid rotor system? (FAA-H-8083-21)

A fully rigid rotor system does not have a flapping hinge; it flaps by actually flexing the blade up and down to compensate for dissymmetry of lift.

E. Blade Flapping and Coning

1. How does coning affect helicopter design?
(FAA-H-8083-21)

The rotation of the rotor system creates centrifugal force (inertia), which tends to pull the blades straight outward from the main rotor hub. The faster the rotation, the greater the centrifugal force. This force gives the rotor blades their rigidity and, in turn, the strength to support the weight of the helicopter.

2. What determines the maximum operating rotor RPM?
(FAA-H-8083-21)

The centrifugal force generated determines the maximum operating rotor RPM due to structural limitations on the main rotor system.

F. Coriolis Effect

1. How does the design of a helicopter compensate for Coriolis effect? (FAA-H-8083-21)

The acceleration and deceleration actions of the rotor blades are absorbed by either dampers or the blade structure itself, depending upon the design of the rotor system.

2. How does a two-bladed rotor system compensate for Coriolis effect? (FAA-H-8083-21)

Two-bladed rotor systems are normally subject to Coriolis effect to a much lesser degree than are articulated rotor systems since the blades are generally "under slung" with respect to the rotor hub, and the change in the distance of the center of mass from the axis of rotation is small. The hunting action is absorbed by the blades through bending. If a two-bladed rotor system is not "under slung," it will be subject to Coriolis effect comparable to that of a fully articulated system.

G. Translating Tendency

1. What are some different ways that the helicopter's design will compensate for translating tendency?

a. Flight controls rigging designed so that the rotor disc is tilted slightly opposite tail rotor thrust when cyclic is centered.

b. Cyclic pitch control system designed with a slight disc tilt opposite tail thrust when at a hover.

c. Main rotor mast is tilted to the left to compensate for translating tendency.

H. Translational Lift

1. How does translational lift affect the helicopter? (FAA-H-8083-21)

When a single-rotor helicopter flies through translational lift, the air flowing through the main rotor and over the tail rotor becomes less turbulent and more aerodynamically efficient.

2. How does translational lift affect the tail rotor? (FAA-H-8083-21)

As the tail rotor efficiency improves, more thrust is produced causing the aircraft to yaw left in a counterclockwise rotor system. It will be necessary to use right torque pedal to correct for this tendency on takeoff.

3. How does translational lift affect the main rotor? (FAA-H-8083-21)

If no corrections are made, the nose rises or pitches up, and rolls to the right. This is caused by combined effects of dissymmetry of lift and transverse flow effect, and is corrected with cyclic control.

I. Pendular Action

1. How does the design of the helicopter affect pendular action? (FAA-H-8083-21)

Since the fuselage of the helicopter, with a single main rotor, is suspended from a single point and has considerable mass, it is free to oscillate either longitudinally or laterally in the same way as a pendulum.

2. What is the cause of pendular action? (FAA-H-8083-21)

Pendular action is caused by the over controlling of the helicopter.

Helicopter
Flight Controls

2

1. What types of helicopters have governors?
(FAA-H-8083-21)

Governors are common on all turbine helicopters and used on some piston-powered helicopters.

2. Why does the introduction of carburetor heat increase manifold pressure and decrease engine power?
(FAA-H-8083-21)

The use of carburetor heat causes a decrease in engine power, sometimes up to 15 percent, because the heated air is less dense than the outside air that had been entering the engine. This enriches the mixture.

Logbooks and Endorsements

3

1. **Is there an endorsement that the student needs to have even before manipulating the controls in an R-22?** (14 CFR Part 61, SFAR 73-1)

Yes, there is an "Awareness Training" that must be conducted by an authorized instructor. It must include the following general subject areas:
- Energy Management
- Mast Bumping
- Low rotor RPM (Blade Stall)
- Low-G hazards
- Rotor RPM

2. **What are all the endorsements concerning SFAR 73?** (14 CFR 61, SFAR 73)

- Prior to flight instruction — Awareness Training Endorsement
- Solo endorsement (in addition to §61.87)
- After the private checkride with less than 200 hours/50 R-22
- Annual endorsement for the rated pilot who does not have 200 hours/50 hours in R-22
- BFR endorsement for the rated pilot who has less than 200 flight hours in a helicopter and more than 50 in the R-22
- BFR endorsement for the rated pilot who has more than 200 flight hours with at least 50 in the R-22

3. **What is an example of the Awareness Training Endorsement?**

I certify that I have given Mr./Ms. _____
the Robinson R22 Helicopter Awareness Training as required by SFAR 73-1 paragraph (2)(a)(3)(i-v) on _____ (date).
Signed: _____

4. What is an example of the SFAR 73 solo endorsement?

I certify that I have given Mr./Ms. _____
all flight and ground instruction as required by the SFAR 73-1
paragraph (2)(b)(3)(I-v) and find him/her proficient to solo the
Robinson R22 helicopter for the next 90 days.
Date: _____ Signed: _____

5. What is an example of an endorsement given after the private checkride SFAR 73-1 annual for rated pilot with less than 200 hours (50 hours in R22)?

I certify that Mr./Ms. _____
has been given annual review specified by SFAR 73-1 paragraph
2(b)(l)(ii) for the Robinson R22 Helicopter and find him/her
proficient to act as pilot in command. A flight review must be
completed by _____ unless the requirements of
paragraph 2(b)(l)(i) are met.
Date: _____ Signed: _____

6. What is an example of an endorsement for SFAR 73-1 rated pilot with less than 200 hours (50 hours in R22)?

I certify that Mr./Ms. _____
has been given training specified by SFAR 73-1 paragraph
2(b)(l)(ii)(A-D) for the Robinson R22 Helicopter and find him/
her proficient to act as pilot in command. A flight review must be
completed by _____ unless the requirements of
paragraph 2(b)(1)(i) are met.
Date: _____ Signed: _____

7. What is an example of an endorsement for a BFR rated pilot with less than 200 hours (50 hours in R22)?

I certify that Mr./Ms. _____,
holder of pilot certificate #_____ has satisfactorily
completed the BFR as required by 14CFR 61.56 in the Robinson
R22 helicopter. A flight review must be completed by_____
unless the requirements of paragraph 2(b)(l)(i) are met.
Date: _____ Signed: _____

8. What is an example of an endorsement for a BFR rated pilot with more than 200 hours (50 hours in R22)?

I certify that Mr./Ms. _____,
holder of pilot certificate #_____ has satisfactorily completed the BFR as required by 14CFR 61.56 in the Robinson R22 helicopter to meet the requirement specified by SFAR 73-1 paragraph 2 (C)(l) on _____.
Date: _____ Signed: _____

Hovering Maneuvers

4

A. Normal Takeoff To a Hover

1. Describe a normal takeoff to a hover.

A normal takeoff to a hover is the process of lifting the helicopter off the ground vertically into the air in a stabilized fashion. The takeoff should be completed with little to no change in attitude or heading as it ascends vertically to a stabilized hover.

2. What are the steps involved in performing a normal takeoff to a hover?

A normal takeoff to a hover can be divided into two steps. The first step is starting the liftoff:

1. Clear left, right, overhead.

2. With cyclic and pedals neutral; increase collective.

3. Pick out a reference 50 to 75 feet ahead and correct sideways or backwards movement as the helicopter lifts.

4. Neutralize yaw with pedals.

5. If helicopter starts moving to the side or rear, lower collective and start over.

The second step is lifting off:

1. As the helicopter lifts, hold heading with pedals and correct the ground track with cyclic.

2. Do a hover check at 3 feet.

3. Once in the hover, make sure power and RPM are within limits (if governor is off stabilize RPM).

3. **What are some of the standards expected of a student for a normal takeoff to a hover?** (FAA-S-8081-16)

   a. Has appropriate knowledge of the maneuver.

   b. Can climb and maintain altitude and then descend in headwind, crosswind and tailwind.

   c. Keeps RPMs within limits.

   d. If within 10 feet of the ground, can hold hovering altitude ±1/2 of that altitude. If more than 10 feet high, can hold altitude ±5 feet.

   e. Avoids conditions that would lead to loss of tail rotor/antitorque effectiveness.

   f. Keeps forward and side movement within 2 feet of chosen point with no aft movement.

   g. Descends vertically to within 2 feet of touchdown point.

   h. Holds heading ±10 degrees.

4. **What are some common student errors when performing a normal takeoff to a hover?** (FAA-S-8081-7A)

   a. Improper RPM control.

   b. Failure to ascend and descend vertically at a suitable rate.

   c. Failure to recognize and correct undesirable drift.

   d. Improper heading control.

   e. Terminating takeoff at an improper altitude.

   f. Over control of collective pitch, cyclic, or anti-torque pedals.

   g. Failure to reduce collective pitch to the full-down position, smoothly and positively, upon surface contact.

B. Surface Taxi

1. Describe a surface taxi.

Surface taxi is a relocation of the helicopter from one point to another along the surface. A surface taxi is used whenever you wish to minimize the effects of rotor downwash.

2. What are the steps involved in performing a surface taxi?

1. Start with helicopter on the ground at hover RPM with collective full down.

2. Move cyclic slightly forward and gradually lift collective to start moving forward on the ground.

3. Pedals control steering and cyclic maintains ground track.

4. Use the cyclic for starting, stopping and taxi speed. Top taxi speed should be a brisk walk.

5. Do not control speed with cyclic. During a crosswind, hold cyclic into the wind to stop any drift.

3. What are some of the standards expected of a student for a surface taxi? (FAA-S-8081-16)

a. Has appropriate knowledge of the maneuver.

b. Surface taxis from point to point with a headwind, crosswind and tailwind while keeping the gear on the ground and avoiding loss of tail rotor effectiveness.

c. Controls taxi speed properly with cyclic, collective and brakes.

d. Properly positions tail wheel, if applicable, locked or unlocked.

e. Keeps RPM within normal limits.

f. Maintains taxi speed appropriate for conditions.

g. Stops within 2 feet of a specified point.

h. Maintains specified track within 2 feet.

4. **What are some common student errors when performing a surface taxi?** (FAA-S-8081-7A)

   a. Improper positioning of cyclic and collective to start and stop movement.

   b. Improper use of brakes.

   c. Taxiing too fast.

   d. Improper use of anti-torque pedals.

C. Hover Taxi

1. Describe a hover taxi.

A forward hovering taxi is normally used to move a helicopter to a specific location, and it is usually begun from a stationary hover. During the maneuver, constant ground speed, altitude, and heading should be maintained.

2. What are the steps involved in performing a hover taxi?

1. Begin from a normal hovering altitude by pushing forward on the cyclic.

2. Once moving, bring cyclic back to neutral to keep the ground-speed at a slow rate—no faster than a brisk walk.

3. Throughout the maneuver, keep a constant ground speed, maintain heading and altitude, and keep proper RPM with throttle.

4. To stop moving forward bring cyclic back until the helicopter stops. Then return cyclic to neutral to stop from going backwards. Forward movement can also be stopped by leveling the helicopter until it drifts to a stop.

3. What are some of the standards expected of a student for a hover taxi? (FAA-S-8081-16)

The applicant must:

1. Have appropriate knowledge of the maneuver.
2. Hover taxi over specified references, demonstrating forward, sideward, and rearward hovering and hovering turns.
3. Maintain RPM within normal limits.
4. Stay within 4 feet of specified ground track.
5. Maintain constant rate of turn at pivot points.
6. Make pivot point turns while staying within 4 feet of correct position.
7. Make 90°, 180°, and 360° pivoting turns, stopping within 10° of specified headings.
8. Within 10 feet of the ground, maintain hovering altitude, ±1/2 of that altitude. If more than 10 feet above the ground, ±5 feet.

4. What are some common student errors when performing a hover taxi? (FAA-S-8081-7A)

a. Improper RPM control.
b. Improper control of heading and track.
c. Erratic altitude control.
d. Misuse of flight controls.

D. Air Taxi

1. Describe an air taxi.

An "air taxi" is best used for longer taxi distances. Because heli-copter pilots are the best judge of the hazards associated with their downwash, they have the responsibility for making sure the operation happens safely. Pilots should notify ATC if taxi instruc-tions need to be amended for safety reasons. The flight should remain below 100 feet AGL and avoid over flying aircraft, vehi-cles and people.

2. What are the steps involved in performing an air taxi?

1. Determine proper airspeed and altitude combination to remain out of the shaded areas of the height/velocity diagram.

2. Watch out for crosswinds that could lead to loss of tail rotor effectiveness.

3. Pick out two references to use for keeping a straight ground track during the maneuver.

4. Begin from a normal hover with forward pressure on the cyclic. Maintain airspeed with the cyclic and control altitude with the collective, and RPM with the throttle.

5. Throughout the maneuver, maintain groundspeed and ground track with the cyclic, hold heading with the pedals, altitude with the collective, and RPM with the throttle. To slow down and stop use aft cyclic and then lower the collective in order to descend to hover altitude.

6. Once forward motion stops, bring cyclic to neutral to stop from going backwards. At the proper hover altitude, increase collec-tive as necessary.

3. What are some of the standards expected of a student for an air taxi? (FAA-S-8081-16)

The student must:

a. Exhibit knowledge of the elements related to air taxiing.

b. Air taxi the helicopter from one point to another under headwind and crosswind conditions.

c. Maintain RPM within normal limits.

d. Select a safe airspeed and altitude considering the possibility of an engine failure during taxi.

e. Maintain desired track and ground speed in headwind and crosswind conditions, avoiding conditions that might lead to loss of tail rotor/anti-torque effectiveness.

f. Maintain a specified altitude, ±10 feet (3 meters).

4. What are some common student errors when performing an air taxi? (FAA-S-8081-7A)

a. Improper RPM control.

b. Erratic altitude and airspeed control.

c. Improper use of collective pitch, cyclic, and anti-torque pedals during operation.

d. Improper use of controls to compensate for wind effect.

E. Slope Operations

1. Describe slope operations.

You usually land a helicopter across the slope rather than with the slope. Landing with the helicopter facing down the slope or downhill is not recommended because of the possibility of striking the tail rotor on the surface.

2. What are the steps involved in performing slope operations?

1. Slope landings—
   - Line up cross-slope facing into the wind at a 3-foot hover.
   - Start a slow descent with the collective.
   - When the upslope skid reaches ground apply cyclic towards uphill skid, holding heading with pedals.
   - Keep lowering the collective while holding the rotor disk level with the horizon until both skids are firmly down.
   - When collective is full down, center cyclic to allow "head clearance" on uphill side.

2. Slope takeoffs (the procedure for a slope takeoff is almost the exact reverse of that for a slope landing)—
   - Apply cyclic toward uphill side and slowly increase collective.
   - As helicopter gets light on the skids, pause and neutralize any movement.
   - Hold heading with pedals and continue increasing collective.
   - As the downhill skid lifts, slowly center cyclic and level the helicopter.
   - Once level, the cyclic should be neutral.
   - While raising off, control ground track with cyclic and use pedals to hold heading until 3-foot hover is reached.

3. **What are some of the standards expected of a student for slope operations?** (FAA-S-8081-16)

The student must:

a. Display appropriate knowledge of the maneuver.

b. Select a suitable slope, approach, and direction considering wind, obstacles, dynamic rollover, and discharging passengers.

c. Properly move toward the slope.

d. Keep RPM within limits.

e. Make a smooth descent to touch the upslope skid on the surface.

f. Maintain positive control while lowering the downslope skid.

g. Recognize a slope that is too steep and abandon the operation before reaching cyclic control stops.

h. Smoothly transition from the slope to a stabilized hover parallel to the ground.

i. Properly move away from the slope.

j. Maintain heading throughout the operation, ±10°.

4. **What are some common student errors when performing slope operations?** (FAA-S-8081-7A)

a. Improper planning for, selection of, approach to, or departure from the slope.

b. Failure to consider wind effects.

c. Improper RPM control.

d. Turning the tail of the helicopter upslope.

e. Lowering downslope skid or wheels too rapidly.

f. Sliding downslope.

g. Improper use of brakes (if applicable).

h. Conditions that, if allowed to develop, may result in dynamic rollover.

Takeoffs, Landings, and Go-Arounds

5

A. Normal Takeoff From a Hover

1. Describe a normal takeoff from a hover.

A normal takeoff from a hover is an orderly transition to forward flight and is executed to increase altitude safely and expeditiously. During the takeoff, fly a profile that avoids the cross-hatched or shaded areas of the height/velocity diagram.

2. What are the steps involved in performing a normal takeoff from a hover?

1. From a 3-foot hover, pick out a reference point(s) to help maintain ground track.

2. Perform 360-degree clearing turn and pretakeoff checks (RPM 104%), warning lights out, instruments green, carb heat as required, hover power (manifold pressure, 3-foot hover height).

3. Use slight forward/left cyclic to start forward (if helicopter settles, increase collective to hold 3 foot altitude), hold heading with pedals.

4. As airspeed increases to about 15 KIAS, ETL will occur— increasing lift and causing the nose to rise.

5. Continue accelerating to 50 KIAS with forward/left cyclic; this will keep the nose down.

6. Add right rudder to compensate for yaw as the higher speed increases tail rotor force.

7. Maintaining ground track and accelerate to 60 KIAS. At 300 feet and 60 knots, keep manifold pressure at climb power (hover power MP).

Continued

Crosswind Considerations:

- During takeoff, climb in a slip to an altitude of 50 feet (place the cyclic into the wind to maintain ground track, use opposite pedal to maintain alignment).
- Above 50 feet, crab into the wind by trimming the aircraft with the pedals and using cyclic to maintain ground track.

3. What are some of the standards expected of a student for a normal takeoff from a hover? (FAA-S-8081-16)

a. Has proper knowledge of the operation and associated performance factors including crosswinds and height/velocity information.

b. Establishes a stationary position on the surface or a stabilized hover, prior to takeoff in headwind and crosswind conditions.

c. Keeps RPM within limits.

d. Accelerates to manufacturer's recommended climb airspeed, ±10 knots.

e. Maintains proper ground track with crosswind correction, if necessary.

f. Remains aware of the possibility of wind shear and/or wake turbulence.

g. Completes checklists, if applicable.

4. What are some common student errors when performing a normal takeoff from a hover? (FAA-S-8081-7A)

a. Improper RPM control.

b. Improper use of cyclic, collective pitch, or anti-torque pedals.

c. Failure to use sufficient power to avoid settling prior to entering effective translational lift.

d. Improper coordination of attitude and power during initial phase of climb-out.

e. Failure to establish and maintain climb power and airspeed.

f. Drift during climb.

B. Max Performance Takeoff

1. Describe a max performance takeoff.

A maximum performance takeoff is used to climb at a steep angle to clear barriers in the flight path. For this kind of takeoff you must thoroughly know the capabilities and limitations of your equipment. You must also consider the wind velocity, temperature, altitude, gross weight, center-of-gravity location, and other factors affecting your technique and the performance of the helicopter.

2. What are the steps involved in performing a max performance takeoff?

a. Before takeoff, check the manifold pressure limit chart for max power available at that altitude and temperature.

b. Clear left, right, above and complete before takeoff checks.

c. Select reference point(s) for ground track alignment.

d. Begin by getting light on the skids, then pause and neutralize movement.

e. Increase collective and position cyclic to break ground and hold a 20 KIAS attitude.

f. Slowly increase collective until maximum power available is reached (this will require substantial left pedal).

g. At 50 feet, lower the nose to a normal 60 KIAS climb attitude.

h. As airspeed passes through 50 KIAS reduce collective to normal climb power (hover power manifold pressure).

i. This takeoff can also be made from a 3-foot hover.

3. **What are some of the standards expected of a student for a max performance takeoff?** (FAA-S-8081-16)

   a. Exhibits knowledge of the elements related to a maximum performance takeoff and climb.

   b. Considers situations where this maneuver is recommended and factors related to takeoff and climb performance, to include height/velocity information.

   c. Maintains RPM within normal limits.

   d. Uses proper control technique to initiate takeoff and forward climb airspeed attitude.

   e. Uses the maximum available takeoff power.

   f. After clearing all obstacles, transitions to normal climb attitude, airspeed, ±10 knots, and power setting.

   g. Remains aware of the possibility of wind shear and/or wake turbulence.

   h. Maintains proper ground track with crosswind correction, if necessary.

   i. Completes the prescribed checklist, if applicable.

4. **What are some common student errors when performing a max performance takeoff?** (FAA-S-8081-7A)

   a. Failure to consider performance data, including height/velocity diagram.

   b. Improper RPM control.

   c. Improper use of cyclic, collective pitch, or anti-torque pedals.

   d. Failure to use the predetermined power setting for establishing attitude and airspeed appropriate to the obstacles to be cleared.

   e. Failure to resume normal climb power and airspeed after obstacle clearance.

   f. Drift during climb.

C. Rolling/Running Takeoff

1. Describe a rolling/running takeoff.

A rolling/running takeoff requires the same technique as the surface taxi. This maneuver is used on helicopters with wheels and when the helicopter may not have enough power to hover, either up at altitude or after a partial power loss. Translational lift can be gained from accelerating across the ground, with the additional lift being created the helicopter could then takeoff normally.

2. What are the steps involved in performing a rolling/running takeoff? (ASA-PHF)

1. Turn the helicopter into the wind and smoothly apply full power while holding the cyclic slightly forward.

2. Once reaching translational lift speed, fly into ground effect and then through translational lift.

3. Use cyclic to correct if there is a pitch down or rolling tendency after liftoff.

4. Use light cyclic pressures since climb power may be limited as the running takeoff is started — otherwise helicopter could settle back to the ground.

5. Best angle of climb speed may be necessary.

3. What are some of the standards expected of a student for a rolling/running takeoff? (FAA-S-8081-16)

a. Has proper knowledge of all related elements of the maneuver.

b. Understands when the maneuver is recommended and has knowledge of performance factors including include height/velocity information.

c. Keeps RPM within limits.

d. Prepares properly for the takeoff.

e. Starts the takeoff by rolling forward along the surface.

f. Transitions to a normal climb airspeed, ±10 knots, and uses correct power setting.

g. Remains aware of the possibility of wind shear and/or wake turbulence.

Continued

   h. Maintains ground track with crosswind correction, if necessary.

   i. Completes the prescribed checklist, if applicable.

4. What are some common student errors when performing a rolling/running takeoff? (FAA-S-8081-7A)

   a. Improper RPM control.

   b. Improper approach angle.

   c. Improper use of cyclic to control rate of closure and collective pitch to control approach angle.

   d. Failure to coordinate pedal corrections with power changes.

   e. Failure to maintain a speed that will take advantage of effective translational lift during final phase of approach.

   f. Touching down at an excessive groundspeed.

   g. Failure to touch down in appropriate attitude.

   h. Failure to maintain directional control after touchdown.

D. Normal Approach

1. Describe a normal approach.

A normal approach is a maneuver in which the helicopter loses altitude at a controlled rate in a controlled attitude.

2. What are the steps involved in performing a normal approach?

   1. At 60 KIAS and 300 feet, head the helicopter into the wind and line up with the touchdown point.

   2. Lower collective to begin descending at a 10–12 degree approach angle.

   3. As the nose pitches down from the decrease in collective, apply aft cyclic.

   4. Use a point on the windshield to match up with the aim point for judging decent angle. If the aim point moves up (relative to windshield spot) angle is too shallow, increase collective. If the aim point moves down, angle is too steep, decrease collective.

5. Use cyclic to control the close-in speed to the aim point.

6. Maintain entry airspeed until apparent ground speed and rate of closure appear to be increasing (should look like a brisk walk).

7. Start decelerating with aft cyclic, maintaining approach angle by reducing collective.

8. Maintain a "brisk walk" rate of closure with cyclic.

9. At about 25 to 40 feet the helicopter will begin to lose ETL (felt as a vibration) and aircraft will settle.

10. Loss of ETL should be anticipated and compensated for with increase of collective—this in turn will cause nose to rise requiring forward cyclic.

11. At about 3 feet, collective should be increased to hold a 3 foot hover. Hold heading with pedals.

12. Any forward movement should be stopped with aft cyclic.

Crosswind Considerations

• Crab into any crosswind on approach and keep in proper trim. At 50 feet start a slip into the wind, keeping the fuselage aligned with the ground track. To establish the slip, apply cyclic into the wind along with opposite pedal.

3. What are some of the standards expected of a student for a normal approach? (FAA-S-8081-16)

a. Shows proper knowledge of elements involved in a normal and crosswind approach.

b. Considers performance data, to include height/velocity information.

c. Considers the wind conditions, landing surface, and obstacles.

d. Selects a suitable termination point.

e. Establishes and maintains the recommended approach angle, and proper rate of closure.

f. Remains aware of the possibility of wind shear and/or wake turbulence.

g. Avoids situations that may result in settling-with-power.

h. Maintains proper ground track with crosswind correction, if necessary.

Continued

    i. Arrives at the termination point, on the surface or at a stabilized hover, ±4 feet).

    j. Completes the prescribed checklist, if applicable.

4. What are some common student errors when performing a normal approach? (FAA-S-8081-7A)

    a. Improper RPM control.

    b. Improper approach angle.

    c. Improper use of cyclic to control rate of closure and collective pitch to control approach angle.

    d. Failure to coordinate pedal corrections with power changes.

    e. Failure to arrive at the termination point at zero groundspeed.

E. Steep Approach

1. Describe a steep approach.

A steep approach is used primarily when there are obstacles in the approach path that are too high to allow a normal approach. A steep approach permits entry into most confined areas and is sometimes used to avoid areas of turbulence around a pinnacle. An approach angle of approximately 15° is considered a steep approach.

2. What are the steps involved in performing a steep approach?

1. At 60 KIAS and 300 feet head the helicopter into the wind and line up with the touchdown point.

2. Lower collective to begin the approach when an approach angle of 15 degrees is intercepted.

3. Coordinate right pedal for trim.

4. Reduce collective more than normal because of the steeper angle.

5. Use the spot on the windshield to judge approach angle.

6. Use aft cyclic to decelerate sooner than on a normal approach.

7. Maintain a crab above 50 feet and a slip below 50 feet.

8. Use collective to control approach angle and rate of descent.

9. Control rate of closure with cyclic and trim with pedals.

10. Loss of ETL will occur higher on a steep approach—collective will need to be increased to prevent settling.

11. Terminate at a stabilized 3-foot hover.

3. What are some of the standards expected of a student for a steep approach? (FAA-S-8081-16)

a. Shows proper knowledge of elements involved in a steep approach.

b. Understands where the maneuver is recommended and has knowledge of the performance factors involved, including height/velocity information.

c. Considers the wind conditions, landing surface, and obstacles.

d. Selects a suitable termination point.

e. Establishes and maintains the recommended approach angle, (15° maximum) and rate of closure.

f. Avoids situations that can result in settling-with-power.

g. Remains aware of the possibility of wind shear and/or wake turbulence.

h. Maintains proper ground track with crosswind correction, if necessary.

i. Arrives at the termination point, on the surface or at a stabilized hover, ±4 feet.

j. Completes the prescribed checklist, if applicable.

4. What are some common student errors when performing a steep approach? (FAA-S-8081-7A)

a. Improper approach angle.

b. Improper RPM control.

c. Improper use of cyclic to control rate of closure and collective pitch to control approach angle.

d. Failure to coordinate pedal corrections with power changes.

e. Failure to arrive at the termination point at zero groundspeed.

f. Inability to determine location where effective translational lift is lost.

F. Running/Roll-On Landing

1. Describe a shallow approach with a running/roll-on landing.

Use a shallow approach and running landing when a high-density altitude prevents a normal or steep approach because of insufficient power to hover. Using a shallow approach and running landing makes use of translational lift until surface contact can be made. If flying a wheeled helicopter, you can also use a roll-on landing to minimize the effect of downwash. The landing area must be smooth and long enough to accommodate a sliding or rolling stop. The glide angle for a shallow approach is approximately 5°.

2. What are the steps involved in performing a shallow approach with a running/roll-on landing?

1. At 60 KIAS and 300 feet, head the helicopter into the wind and line up with the touchdown point.

2. Lower collective to begin the approach when an approach angle of 5 degrees is intercepted.

3. Maintain entry airspeed until apparent rate of closure and groundspeed appear to be increasing.

4. Begin slow deceleration with aft cyclic.

5. Maintain approach angle with collective, keep aircraft in trim.

6. Plan to arrive at touchdown point at an airspeed that will take advantage of ETL during surface contact with landing gear parallel to the ground.

7. Helicopter should be level prior to ground contact.

8. Once on the ground, control heading with pedals, ground track with cyclic, and do not lower collective rapidly for braking action.

Crosswind Considerations
Just like with a normal and steep approach, use a crab above 50 feet AGL and a slip below 50 feet AGL to keep the aircraft lined up with the ground track.

3. **What are some of the standards expected of a student for a shallow approach with a running/roll-on landing?** (FAA-S-8081-16)

a. Has appropriate knowledge of the maneuver including its purpose, and understands performance factors such as height/velocity information and effect of landing surface texture.

b. Maintains RPM within normal limits.

c. Considers obstacles and other hazards.

d. Establishes and maintains the recommended approach angle, and proper rate of closure.

e. Remains aware of the possibility of wind shear and/or wake turbulence.

f. Maintains proper ground track with crosswind correction, if necessary.

g. Maintains a speed that will take advantage of effective translational lift during surface contact with landing gear parallel with the ground track.

h. Uses proper flight control technique after surface contact.

i. Completes the prescribed checklist, if applicable.

4. **What are some common student errors when performing a shallow approach with a running/roll-on landing?** (FAA-S-8081-7A)

a. Improper RPM control.

b. Improper approach angle.

c. Improper use of cyclic to control rate of closure and collective pitch to control approach angle.

d. Failure to coordinate pedal corrections with power changes.

e. Failure to maintain a speed that will take advantage of effective translational lift during final phase of approach.

f. Touching down at an excessive groundspeed.

g. Failure to touch down in appropriate attitude.

h. Failure to maintain directional control after touchdown.

G. Go-Around

1. Describe a go-around.

A go-around is used to abort any approach where a safe landing is not assured. Go-arounds should be handled expediently in case the cause of the go-around is sudden.

2. What are the steps involved in performing a go-around?

Anytime the pilot feels an approach is uncomfortable, incorrect, or potentially dangerous, it should be abandoned. The decision to make a go-around should be positive and initiated before a critical situation develops. When the decision is made, carry it out without hesitation. When you initiate the go-around, increase the collective to takeoff power to stop the descent and to establish a climb. Use pedal to control heading and cyclic to adjust airspeed to 60 KIAS. Maintain proper ground track with crosswind correction if necessary.

3. What are some of the standards expected of a student for a go-around? (FAA-S-8081-16)

a. Exhibits knowledge of the elements related to a go-around and when it is necessary.

b. Makes a timely decision to discontinue the approach to landing.

c. Maintains RPM within normal limits.

d. Establishes proper control input to stop descent and initiate climb.

e. Retracts the landing gear, if applicable, after a positive rate of climb indication.

f. Maintains proper ground track with crosswind correction, if necessary.

g. Transitions to a normal climb airspeed, ±10 knots.

h. Completes the prescribed checklist, if applicable.

4. What are some common student errors when performing a go-around? (FAA-S-8081-7A)

a. Failure to recognize a situation where a go-around is necessary.

b. Improper application of flight controls during transition to climb attitude.

c. Failure to control drift and clear obstacles safely.

Fundamentals of Flight

6

A. Straight-and-Level Flight

1. Describe straight-and-level flight.

Straight-and-level flight is flight in which a constant altitude and heading are maintained. The attitude of the helicopter determines the airspeed and is controlled by the cyclic. Altitude is primarily controlled by use of the collective.

2. What are the steps involved in performing straight-and-level flight?

A level flight attitude is best determined by referencing the horizon with a fixed point in the cockpit, such as the magnetic compass or the tip-path plane. (Attitude/pitch control is the most important aspect of straight and level flight.)

1. Detect changes in attitude by noting changes between the fixed point and the horizon.

2. Airspeed is determined by attitude and controlled by the cyclic.

3. The cyclic control is very sensitive and requires very slight pressure to effect change.

4. Normal cruise speed for training is 70 KIAS (R22).

5. The collective controls cruise power (manifold pressure) and altitude.

6. Each collective adjustment requires pedal to keep in trim (increase requires left pedal, decrease requires right pedal).

7. An increase in collective causes the nose to rise, which requires slight forward cyclic to stay level. The opposite is true with a decrease in collective—the nose will drop, requiring aft cyclic.

3. **What are some of the standards expected of a student for a straight-and-level flight?** (FAA-S-8081-16)

Performance Standards:	Private	Commercial
Airspeed	±10 KIAS	±5 KIAS
Altitude	±100 feet	±50 feet
Heading	±10°	±5°

4. **What are some common student errors when performing straight-and-level flight?** (FAA-S-8081-7A)

   a. Improper coordination of flight controls.

   b. Failure to cross-check and correctly interpret outside and instrument references.

   c. Faulty trim technique.

B. Level Turns

1. **Describe level turns.**

   To turn the aircraft using a constant angle of bank at a constant airspeed while maintaining altitude.

2. **What are the steps involved in performing a level turn?**

   1. From straight and level (70 KIAS) clear in the direction of the turn.

   2. Smoothly apply cyclic in direction of turn until reaching desired angle of bank.

   3. Do not use pedals to assist the turn.

   4. Use horizon as a reference for 70 KIAS attitude, control angle of bank with cyclic.

   5. As bank increases, increase collective to hold altitude.

   6. Keep in trim with pedals.

   7. To roll out, apply cyclic opposite the turn and reduce collective to cruise power (if it was added); remain in trim.

3. **What are some of the standards expected of a student for level turns?** (FAA-S-8081-16)

Performance Standards:	Private	Commercial
Airspeed	±10 KIAS	±5 KIAS
Altitude	±100 feet	±50 feet
Roll-Out Heading	±10°	±5°

4. **What are some common student errors when performing level turns?** (FAA-S-8081-7A)

   a. Improper coordination of flight controls.

   b. Failure to cross-check and correctly interpret outside and instrument references.

   c. Faulty trim technique.

C. Normal Climbs

1. **Describe a normal climb.**

   A normal climb is a controlled change of altitude at a stabilized rate, within normal operating limits.

2. **What are the steps involved in performing a normal climb?**

   1. Start by applying aft cyclic to obtain the approximate climb attitude.

   2. Simultaneously increase the collective and throttle to obtain climb power and maintain RPM.

   3. Use left pedal (counterclockwise rotor) to compensate for increased torque.

   4. Adjust cyclic to hold normal climb airspeed.

   5. Maintain climb attitude, heading, airspeed with cyclic.

   6. Maintain climb power and RPM with the collective and throttle.

   7. Use anti-torque pedals for longitudinal trim.

Continued

8. To level off, start adjusting the attitude to level flight attitude (forward cyclic) a few feet prior to reaching the desired altitude (generally lead by 10% of climb rate — e.g., lead by 50 feet for a 500 fpm climb).

9. Maintain climb power until reaching cruising airspeed.

10. Adjust collective for cruising power and set throttle for cruise RPM.

11. Maintain longitudinal trim and heading with pedals during level-off.

3. What are some of the standards expected of a student for a normal climbs? (FAA-S-8081-16)

Performance Standards:	Private	Commercial
Airspeed	±10 KIAS	±5 KIAS
Level Off Altitude	±100 feet	±50 feet
Heading	±10°	±5°

4. What are some common student errors when performing a normal climbs? (FAA-S-8081-7A)

a. Improper coordination of flight controls.

b. Failure to cross-check and correctly interpret outside and instrument references.

c. Faulty trim technique.

D. Normal Descent

1. Describe a normal descent.

A normal descent is a decrease in altitude at a controlled rate in a controlled attitude.

2. What are the steps involved in performing a normal descent?

1. Normally for training 60 KIAS is used for a descent speed and 500 fpm for rate of descent.

2. Start from straight and level (70 KIAS) by clearing below the aircraft.

3. Decrease collective about 4–5 inches of manifold pressure below cruise setting (this will provide 500 fpm at 60 KIAS).

4. Remain in trim with right pedal.

5. Use aft cyclic to hold 60 KIAS attitude.

6. 50 feet above level off altitude, begin increasing collective to 1 inch above cruise power until speed reaches 70 KIAS.

7. Adjust power to hold 70 KIAS, remain in trim with left pedal.

8. Continually cross-check outside references (attitude and heading) with inside reference (flight instruments).

3. What are some of the standards expected of a student for a normal descent? (FAA-S-8081-16)

Performance Standards:	Private	Commercial
Airspeed	±10 KIAS	±5 KIAS
Level-off Altitude	±100 feet	±50 feet
Heading	±10°	±5°

4. What are some common student errors when performing a normal descent? (FAA-S-8081-7A)

a. Improper coordination of flight controls.

b. Failure to cross-check and correctly interpret outside and instrument references.

c. Faulty trim technique.

Performance Maneuvers

7

A. Rapid Deceleration (Quick Stop)

1. Describe a rapid deceleration (quick stop).

The rapid deceleration or quick stop maneuver is used to slow the helicopter rapidly and bring it to a stationary hover. The maneuver requires a high degree of coordination of all controls. It is practiced at an altitude that permits a safe clearance between the tail rotor and the surface throughout the maneuver, especially at the point where the pitch attitude is highest. The altitude at completion should be no higher than the maximum safe hovering altitude prescribed by the manufacturer. In selecting an altitude at which to begin the maneuver, you should take into account the overall length of the helicopter and the height/velocity diagram. Even though the maneuver is called a rapid deceleration or quick stop, it is performed slowly and smoothly with the primary emphasis on coordination.

2. What are the steps involved in performing a rapid deceleration?

1. Perform a normal takeoff into the wind.

2. At a minimum altitude of 40 feet, apply forward cyclic to accelerate to 30–40 KIAS (maintain altitude).

3. Begin the quick stop by smoothly lowering the collective, adding right pedal, and simultaneously applying aft cyclic to decelerate.

4. Apply aft cyclic as needed to maintain entry altitude throughout the deceleration.

5. As airspeed is lost, the helicopter will begin to settle. Slowly increase the collective to control the angle and rate of descent by adding forward cyclic to level the helicopter. Angle of descent should be no greater than a steep approach.

6. Maintain heading with pedals, and terminate at a stabilized 3-foot hover. Use caution to avoid terminating at a high hover or in an extreme tail low attitude.

Caution: The quick stop should only be performed into the wind, as there is a high risk of settling with power in a downwind condition.

3. What are some of the standards expected of a student for a rapid deceleration? (FAA-S-8081-16)

a. Exhibits knowledge of the elements related to rapid deceleration.

b. Maintains RPM within normal limits.

c. Properly coordinates all controls throughout the maneuver.

d. Maintains an altitude that permits safe clearance between the tail boom and the surface.

e. Decelerates and terminates in a stationary hover at the recommended hovering altitude.

f. Maintains heading throughout the maneuver, ±10°.

4. What are some common student errors when performing a rapid deceleration? (FAA-S-8081-7A)

a. Improper RPM control.

b. Improper use of anti-torque pedals.

c. Improper coordination of cyclic and collective controls.

d. Failure to properly control the rate of deceleration.

e. Stopping of forward motion in a tail-low attitude.

f. Failure to maintain safe clearance over terrain.

B. Straight-In Autorotation

1. Describe a straight-in autorotation.

In a helicopter, an autorotation is a descending maneuver where the engine is disengaged from the main rotor system and the rotor blades are driven solely by the upward flow of air through the rotor. In other words, the engine is no longer supplying power to the main rotor.

2. What are the steps involved in performing a straight-in autorotation with a power recovery?

The Entry

1. Turn governor off. Then, from level flight of 70 KIAS, at or above 500 feet AGL, and headed into the wind, smoothly but firmly lower the collective full down without reducing the throttle.

2. Coordinate the collective movement with right pedal for trim and aft cyclic to establish a 65 KIAS attitude. The RPM needles will usually split, establishing an autorotative descent. If the needles do not split, reduce the throttle slightly.

3. Cross-check attitude, trim, rotor RPM and airspeed. A slight increase in collective will be necessary to maintain rotor RPM in the green. The throttle should be retarded to maintain the engine RPM at idle.

The Glide

1. Establish descent at 65 KIAS (maintain this attitude throughout glide).

2. Maintain altitude during glide.

3. Aft cyclic will cause increase in RPM (straight-in autorotation); this should be controlled with increased collective.

4. If collective is increased to control RPM, reduce throttle slightly to prevent correlator from joining the needles.

5. Avoid a large collective increase which will result in a rapid decay of rotor RPM and lead to "chasing RPM."

Continued

6. Keep rotor RPM in the green, keep aircraft in trim during glide.
7. Below 100 feet AGL, use slip to stay aligned.
8. Hold 65 KIATs attitude with cyclic, avoid looking straight down in front of aircraft.
9. Keep cross-checking attitude, trim, rotor RPM, airspeed.

Note—
As the aircraft descends through 100 feet AGL, make an immediate power recovery if the following conditions **do not** exist:

- Rotor RPM in the green
- Airspeed 50 KIAS minimum

The Flare

1. Begin the flare at about 40 feet with cyclic to reduce forward airspeed and to decrease rate of descent.
2. The amount of flare will depend on wind conditions and gross weight, and should gradually be increased so that groundspeed and rate of descent are significantly decreased.
3. Too much flare will cause the helicopter to balloon up, causing a high vertical descent, as airspeed is lost.

The Power Recovery

1. At a skid height of approximately 8 to 10 feet, begin to level the helicopter with forward cyclic.
2. Extreme caution should be used to avoid an excessive nose high/tail low attitude below 10 feet. Just prior to achieving a level attitude, with the nose still slightly up, increase the throttle and collective while using left pedal to maintain heading.
3. As the RPM needles join, it may be necessary to add throttle to achieve a hover and maintain 104% RPM. Do not allow the helicopter to descend below 3 feet during the power recovery.

3. **What are some of the standards expected of a student for a straight-in autorotation with a power recovery?** (FAA-S-8081-16)

   a. Exhibits knowledge of the elements related to a straight-in autorotation terminating with a power recovery to a hover.

   b. Selects a suitable touchdown area.

   c. Initiates the maneuver at the proper point.

   d. Establishes proper aircraft trim and autorotation airspeed, ±5 knots.

   e. Maintains rotor RPM within normal limits.

   f. Compensates for wind speed and direction as necessary to avoid undershooting or overshooting the selected landing area.

   g. Uses proper deceleration, collective pitch application to a hover.

   h. Comes to a hover within 100 feet (30 meters) of a designated point.

4. **What are some common student errors when performing a straight-in autorotation with a power recovery?** (FAA-S-8081-7A)

   a. Improper engine and rotor RPM control.

   b. Uncoordinated use of flight controls, particularly anti-torque pedals.

   c. Improper attitude and airspeed during descent.

   d. Improper judgment and technique during termination.

C. 180° Autorotation

1. **Describe a 180° autorotation with a power recovery.**

   A turn, or a series of turns, can be made during an autorotation in order to land into the wind or avoid obstacles. The turn is usually made early so that the remainder of the autorotation is the same as a straight-in autorotation.

2. What are the steps involved in performing a 180° autorotation with a power recovery?

The Entry

1. Establish the aircraft on downwind at 70 KIAS and 700 feet AGL.

2. Turn the governor off.

3. When abeam the intended touchdown point, enter the autorotation by smoothly, but firmly, lowering the collective full down without reducing the throttle. Usually the needles will split establishing an autorotation. If the needles do not split, reduce the throttle slightly.

4. Apply right pedal for trim and aft cyclic to establish a 65 KIAS attitude. Cross-check attitude, trim, rotor RPM, and airspeed.

The Glide/Turn

1. Establish glide attitude for 65 KIAS then begin a 180-degree turn.

2. The proper angle of bank will be determined by wind velocity, but use caution to avoid an excessively steep turn. Throughout the turn, maintain the proper attitude (airspeed) and keep the aircraft in trim.

3. Changes in the aircraft's attitude and the angle of bank will cause corresponding increases and decreases in rotor RPM.

4. Adjust the collective in the turn to maintain rotor RPM in the green: up collective to lower RPM, down collective to raise RPM.

5. Continually cross-check the rotor RPM when maneuvering in autorotative turns as the low inertia rotor system can allow rapid increases in rotor RPM.

6. The turn should be completed and the helicopter aligned with the intended touchdown area prior to passing through 100 feet AGL. If the collective has been increased to load the rotor during the turn, it must to be lowered on roll-out to prevent decay in RPM.

Note—
As the aircraft descends through 100 feet AGL, make an immediate power recovery if the following conditions **do not** exist:
- Aircraft aligned with the touchdown point
- Rotor RPM in the green
- Airspeed 50 KIAS minimum
- The flare—Same as straight-in autorotation
- Power recovery—Same as straight-in autorotation

The Flare
Use the same flare technique as used in a straight-in autorotation.

The Power Recovery
Use the same power recovery as used in a straight-in autorotation.

3. **What are some of the standards expected of a student for a 180° autorotation with a power recovery?** (FAA-S-8081-16)

Use the same standards as used for a straight-in autorotation except the hover should be brought to within 50 feet of a designated point.

4. **What are some common student errors when performing a 180° autorotation with a power recovery?** (FAA-S-8081-7A)

a. Improper engine and rotor RPM control.

b. Uncoordinated use of flight controls, particularly anti-torque pedals.

c. Improper attitude and airspeed during descent.

d. Improper judgment and technique during the termination.

Emergency Operations

8

A. Power Failure at a Hover

1. Describe a power failure at a hover.

Power failures in a hover, also called hovering autorotations, are practiced so that you automatically make the correct response when confronted with engine stoppage or certain other emergencies while hovering.

2. What are the steps involved in performing a power failure at a hover?

1. Begin from a stabilized 3 foot hover at 104% RPM, governor off, over level terrain and headed into the wind.

2. If necessary, reposition the left hand so that the throttle can easily be rolled off into the override position.

3. Firmly roll the throttle into the spring-loaded override while simultaneously adding right pedal to maintain heading. The loss of tail rotor thrust will cause a left drift when the throttle is rolled off. Compensate for this drift with right cyclic.

4. Use caution not to raise or lower the collective when rolling off the throttle. When the aircraft has settled to approximately 1 foot, fully increase the collective, holding the throttle firmly in the spring-loaded override to cushion the landing. As the skids touch down, apply slight forward cyclic. Once firmly on the ground, lower the collective full down.

Caution: Avoid any sideward or rearward movement on touchdown to prevent the possibility of a rollover.

3. **What are some of the standards expected of a student for a power failure at a hover?** (FAA-S-8081-16)

   a. Exhibits knowledge of the elements related to power failure at a hover.

   b. Determines that the terrain below the aircraft is suitable for a safe touchdown.

   c. Performs autorotation from a stationary or forward hover into the wind at recommended altitude, and RPM, while maintaining established heading, ±10°.

   d. Touches down with minimum sideward movement, and no rearward movement.

   e. Exhibits orientation, division of attention, and proper planning.

4. **What are some common student errors when performing a power failure at a hover?** (FAA-S-8081-7A)

   a. Failure to apply correct and adequate pedal when power is reduced.

   b. Failure to correct drift prior to touchdown.

   c. Improper application of collective pitch.

   d. Failure to touch down in a level attitude.

B. Power Failure at Altitude

1. Describe a power failure at altitude (forced landing).

Power failure at altitude or forced landing is where the instructor will simulate an emergency situation designed to develop the student's reaction time, planning and judgment in case of an actual power failure.

2. What are the steps involved in performing a power failure at altitude (forced landing)?

During cruise flight with the student at the controls, the instructor will initiate the forced landing by announcing "engine failure" and rolling the throttle to the idle position. The student will immediately execute the following procedures:

1. Lower the collective full down and coordinate the right pedal for trim, and aft cyclic to maintain attitude. This should be accomplished quick enough to prevent the rotor RPM from decaying below 90%.

2. As the rotor RPM builds back into the green, increase collective as necessary to maintain rotor RPM in the green (keep the throttle against in idle position).

3. Once established in an autorotative descent, select an intended landing area. Maneuver the helicopter as necessary to align the aircraft with the intended landing area, generally headed into the wind.

4. Use changes of the collective and cyclic, if necessary, to maintain the rotor RPM in green arc while maneuvering. Airspeed should be adjusted to 65 KIAS.

5. Prior to passing through 100 feet, the aircraft should be aligned with the touchdown area, at 65 KIAS, with rotor RPM in the green, and the aircraft in trim. Execute a termination with power as with a straight-in autorotation or an immediate power recovery as directed by the instructor.

3. **What are some of the standards expected of a student for a power failure at altitude?** (FAA-S-8081-16)

   a. Exhibits knowledge of the elements related to power failure at altitude.

   b. Establishes an autorotation and selects a suitable landing area.

   c. Establishes proper aircraft trim and autorotation airspeed, ±5 knots.

   d. Maintains rotor RPM within normal limits.

   e. Compensates for windspeed and direction as necessary to avoid undershooting or overshooting the selected landing area.

   f. Terminates approach with a power recovery at a safe altitude when directed by the examiner.

4. **What are some common student errors when performing a power failure at altitude?** (FAA-S-8081-7A)

   a. Failure to promptly recognize the emergency, establish and maintain proper rotor RPM, and confirm engine condition.

   b. Improper judgment in selection of a landing area.

   c. Failure to estimate approximate wind direction and speed.

   d. Uncoordinated use of flight controls during autorotation entry and descent.

   e. Improper attitude and airspeed during autorotation entry and descent.

   f. Failure to fly the most suitable pattern for existing situation.

   g. Failure to accomplish the emergency procedure, as time permits.

   h. Undershooting or overshooting selected landing area.

   i. Uncoordinated use of flight controls during power recovery.

C. Vortex Ring State (Settling With Power)

1. Describe vortex ring state (settling with power).

Vortex ring state describes an aerodynamic condition where a helicopter may be in a vertical descent with up to maximum power applied, and little or no cyclic authority. The term "settling with power" comes from the fact that the helicopter keeps settling even though full engine power is applied.

2. What are the steps involved in practicing settling with power?

1. From a stabilized OGE hover, begin to lower the collective so as to establish a sink rate of at least 300 FPM or more.

2. The aircraft will begin to shudder. This is the beginning of settling with power. Application of additional up collective will increase the vibration and sink rate. Once the condition is well developed, a rate of sink in excess of 2,000 FPM *can* result. Recovery should be initiated at the first sign.

3. To recover, apply forward cyclic to increase airspeed and simultaneously reduce the collective (if altitude permits).

4. The recovery is complete when the aircraft passes through effective translational lift and a normal climb is established.

3. What are some of the standards expected of a student for settling with power? (FAA-S-8081-16)

a. Exhibits knowledge of the elements related to settling with power.

b. Selects an altitude that will allow recovery to be completed no less than 1,000 feet (300 meters) AGL or, if applicable, the manufacturer's recommended altitude, whichever is higher.

c. Promptly recognizes and announces the onset of settling with power.

d. Uses the appropriate recovery procedure.

4. **What are some common student errors when practicing settling with power?** (FAA-S-8081-7A)

a. Failures to recognize conditions that are conducive to development of settling with power.

b. Failure to detect first indications of settling with power.

c. Improper use of controls during recovery.

D. Low RPM Recovery

1. Describe a low RPM recovery.

Under certain conditions of high weight, high temperature, or high-density altitude, you might get into a situation where the RPM is low even though you are using maximum throttle. This is usually the result of the main rotor blades having an angle of attack that has created so much drag that engine power is not sufficient to maintain or attain normal operating RPM.

2. What are the steps involved in practicing a low RPM recovery?

During takeoff, cruise flight, high altitude, and maximum performance climbs at 104% RPM, the instructor turns the governor off and slowly decreases the throttle to 95% RPM. The low RPM condition will be recognized by:

a. A noticeable decrease in engine noise.

b. Aircraft vibration and cyclic stick shake at higher airspeeds.

c. The low rotor RPM warning horn and light will engage at approximately 97% RPM.

d. The instructor should demonstrate the further increase in vibration and decrease in engine noise by decreasing the RPM to 90% RPM.

Upon recognizing the low RPM condition, simultaneously add throttle and lower the collective to regain operating RPM. A gentle aft cyclic movement will help the recovery, but the primary recovery controls are the collective and throttle. Avoid any forward cyclic input, which will inhibit RPM recovery. Once RPM is regained, slowly raise the collective to reduce the sink rate while closely monitoring the RPM.

3. **What are some of the standards expected of a student for a low RPM recovery?** (FAA-S-8081-16)

   a. Exhibits knowledge of the elements related to low rotor RPM recovery, including the combination of conditions that are likely to lead to this situation.

   b. Detects the development of low rotor RPM and initiates prompt corrective action.

   c. Uses the appropriate recovery procedure.

4. **What are some common student errors when performing a low RPM recovery?** (FAA-S-8081-7A)

   a. Failure to recognize conditions that are conducive to the development of low rotor RPM.

   b. Failure to detect the development of low rotor RPM and to initiate prompt corrective action.

   c. Improper use of controls.

E. Anti-Torque System Failure

1. **Describe an anti-torque system failure.**

Anti-torque failures usually fall into two categories. One focuses on failure of the power drive portion of the tail rotor system resulting in a complete loss of anti-torque. The other category covers mechanical control failures where the pilot is unable to change or control tail rotor thrust even though the tail rotor may still be providing anti-torque thrust.

2. **What are the steps involved in performing an anti-torque system failure in a hover?**

The failure is usually indicated by a right yaw that cannot be stopped by applying left pedal. However to practice or simulate this, the instructor should apply right pedal to increase rate of turn. Only a qualified instructor should demonstrate this maneuver. When the helicopter accelerates to the right, immediately close throttle and perform a hovering power-off landing autorotation. Keep the helicopter level and increase collective just before touchdown to cushion landing.

3. What are the steps involved in performing an anti-torque system failure in forward flight?

Complete loss of tail rotor function and its component parts is the most serious form of tail rotor failure. It is usually indicated by a right yaw and extremely nose-low attitude because of the change of C.G. Immediately close the throttle and perform an autorotation. The throttle may be used to keep the nose of the helicopter straight just prior to touchdown.

4. What are the steps involved in performing stuck right, left, or neutral pedals in forward flight?

This malfunction can occur if the pedal controls between the tail rotor gearbox and the pedals jam or break. The tail rotor blades will be operating normally in whichever position they're stuck in and the pitch cannot be changed. The procedure for landing is a shallow approach running landing using the following procedures:

1. Make shallow turns and minimize collective and throttle movements to prevent excessive yawing.

2. Just prior to ground contact, use throttle and/or airspeed to align nose of helicopter in direction of landing.

3. Continue to use throttle for directional control in a stuck right or neutral pedal situation until the helicopter does come to a complete stop.

4. In the case of stuck left, use the collective to align nose of the helicopter with the ground track.

5. What are some of the standards expected of a student flight instructor for a anti-torque system failure? (FAA-S-8081-16)

Exhibits instructional knowledge of the elements related to low rotor RPM recovery by describing—

a. Conditions that are likely to result in low rotor RPM.

b. Potential problems from low rotor RPM if a timely correction is not made.

c. Techniques for recovery.

Exhibits instructional knowledge of common errors related to low rotor RPM recovery by describing—

a. Failure to recognize conditions that are conducive to the development of low rotor RPM.

b. Failure to detect the development of low rotor RPM and to initiate prompt corrective action.

c. Improper use of controls.

6. What are some common student errors when performing an anti-torque system failure? (FAA-S-8081-7A)

a. Failure to recognize conditions that are conducive to the development of low rotor RPM.

b. Failure to detect the development of low rotor RPM and to initiate prompt corrective action.

c. Improper use of controls.

F. Dynamic Rollover

1. Describe a dynamic rollover.

Dynamic rollover is the helicopter's tendency to continue rolling when the critical angle is exceeded. It begins when the helicopter starts to pivot around its skid or wheel.

2. What are the steps involved in recovery from dynamic rollover?

Dynamic rollover cannot be stopped by application of opposite cyclic control alone. You should quickly lower the collective to stop dynamic rollover from developing.

3. What are some of the standards of knowledge expected of a student for a dynamic rollover? (FAA-S-8081-7A)

a. Exhibits knowledge of the elements related to the aerodynamics of dynamic rollover.

b. Understands the interaction between the anti-torque thrust, crosswind, slope, CG, cyclic and collective pitch control in contributing to dynamic rollover.

c. Explains preventive flight technique during takeoffs, landings, and slope operations.

4. What are some of the instructor requirements for knowledge of dynamic rollover? (FAA-S-8081-7A)

a. Helicopter aerodynamics involved.

b. How interaction between anti-torque thrust, crosswind, slope, cyclic and collective pitch control contribute to dynamic rollover.

c. Preventive actions used for takeoffs and landings on different surfaces.

G. Ground Resonance

1. Describe ground resonance.

Ground resonance is an aerodynamic phenomenon associated with fully-articulated rotor systems. It develops when the rotor blades move out of phase with each other and cause the rotor disc to become unbalanced. This condition can cause a helicopter to self-destruct in a matter of seconds. However, for this condition to occur, the helicopter must be in contact with the ground. If you allow your helicopter to touch down firmly on one corner (wheel-type landing gear is most conducive for this) the shock is transmitted to the main rotor system. This may cause the blades to move out of their normal relationship with each other. This movement occurs along the drag hinge.

2. What is the corrective action to stop ground resonance?

If the RPM is in the normal operating range, you should fly the helicopter off the ground, and allow the blades to automatically realign themselves. You can then make a normal touchdown. If the RPM is low, the corrective action to stop ground resonance is close the throttle and immediately and fully lower the collective to place the blades in low pitch.

3. What are some of the standards of knowledge expected of a student for ground resonance? (FAA-S-8081-16)

a. Exhibits knowledge of the elements related to a fully articulated rotor system and the aerodynamics of ground resonance.

b. Understands the conditions that contribute to ground resonance.

c. Explains preventive flight technique during takeoffs and landings.

4. What are some instructor requirements for knowledge of ground resonance? (FAA-S-8081-7A)

a. Aerodynamics involved and association with a fully articulated rotor system.

b. Conditions that are conducive to the development of ground resonance.

c. Preventive actions used for takeoffs and landings on different surfaces.

H. Low-G Conditions

1. Describe low-G conditions.

Pushing the cyclic control forward abruptly from either straight-and-level flight or after a climb can put the helicopter into a low-G (weightless) flight condition. During the low-G condition, the lateral cyclic has little, if any, effect because the rotor thrust has been reduced. In a counterclockwise rotor system (clockwise would be the reverse), there is no main rotor thrust component to the left to counteract the tail rotor to the right, and since the tail rotor is above the CG, the tail rotor thrust causes the helicopter to roll rapidly to the right. If you attempt to stop the right roll by applying full left cyclic before regaining main rotor thrust, the rotor can exceed its flapping limits and cause structural failure of the rotor shaft due to mast bumping, or it may allow a blade to contact the airframe.

2. What is the corrective action upon recognition of a low-G condition?

If you do find yourself in a low-G condition, which can be recognized by a feeling of weightlessness and an uncontrolled roll to the right, you should immediately and smoothly apply aft cyclic. Do not attempt to correct the rolling action with lateral cyclic. By applying aft cyclic, you will load the rotor system, which in turn produces thrust. Once thrust is restored, left cyclic control becomes effective, and you can roll the helicopter to a level attitude.

3. **What are some of the standards of knowledge expected of a student for low-G conditions?** (FAA-S-8081-16)

   a. Exhibits knowledge of the elements related to low-G conditions.

   b. Understands and recognizes the situations that contribute to low-G conditions.

   c. Explains proper recovery procedures.

4. **What are some instructor requirements for knowledge of a low-G condition?** (FAA-S-8081-7A)

   a. Situations that will cause a low-G condition.

   b. Recognition of low-G conditions.

   c. Proper recovery procedures to prevent mast bumping.

   d. Effects of this condition on different types of rotor systems.

Special Operations

9

A. High, Low, Ground Reconnaissance

1. Describe a high reconnaissance.

The purpose of a high reconnaissance is to determine the wind direction and speed, a point for touchdown, the suitability of the landing area, the approach and departure axes, obstacles and their effect on wind patterns, and the most suitable flight paths into and out of the area. When conducting a high reconnaissance, give particular consideration to forced landing areas in case of an emergency.

2. Describe a low reconnaissance.

A low reconnaissance is accomplished during the approach to the landing area. When flying the approach, verify what was observed in the high reconnaissance, and check for anything new that may have been missed at a higher altitude, such as wires, slopes, and small crevices. If everything is all right, you can complete the approach to a landing. However, you must make the decision to land or go-around before effective translational lift is lost.

3. Describe a ground reconnaissance.

Prior to departing an unfamiliar location, make a detailed analysis of the area. There are several factors to consider during this evaluation. Besides determining the best departure path, you must select a route that will get your helicopter from its present position to the takeoff point.

B. Confined Area Operation

1. Describe a confined area operation.

A confined area is an area where the flight of the helicopter is limited in some direction by terrain or the presence of obstructions, natural or manmade. For example, a clearing in the woods, a city street, a road, a building roof, etc., can each be regarded as a confined area. Generally, takeoffs and landings should be made into the wind to obtain maximum airspeed with minimum groundspeed.

2. What are the steps involved in performing confined area operation?

Approach and Landing

Begin with a high reconnaissance to determine suitability landing area—normally at 500 feet and 60 KIAS.

1. Consider the wind direction and speed; the most suitable flight-paths into and out of the area with particular consideration being given to forced landing areas; determine the size of barriers and select a point of touchdown.

2. A low reconnaissance will be necessary to verify what was seen in the high reconnaissance.

3. The approach should be as close to normal as possible. The approach angle should be steep enough to permit clearance of the barrier, but normally not greater than a steep approach angle. The decision to make the landing or go-around must be made before passing the barrier/obstacle.

4. Terminate the approach to the ground if surface conditions permit.

Takeoff

1. Ground reconnaissance should be conducted before takeoff to determine the point from which the takeoff should be initiated; wind condition and how best to get from the landing point to the proposed takeoff position. This reconnaissance can be made from the cockpit or by conducting a walk around the area.

2. Perform pretakeoff checks and clear aircraft left, right and overhead.

3. Use a maximum performance takeoff to clear barriers. After clearing barriers, reduce power to a normal climb airspeed and rate of climb.

3. What are some of the standards expected of a student for confined area operation? (FAA-S-8081-16)

a. Exhibits knowledge of the elements related to confined area operations.

b. Accomplishes a proper high and low reconnaissance.

c. Selects a suitable approach path, termination point, and departure path.

d. Tracks the selected approach path at an acceptable approach angle and rate of closure to the termination point.

e. Maintains RPM within normal limits.

f. Avoids situations that can result in settling-with-power.

g. Terminates at a hover or on the surface as conditions allow.

h. Accomplishes a proper ground reconnaissance.

i. Selects a suitable takeoff point, considers factors affecting takeoff and climb performance under various conditions.

4. What are some common student errors when performing confined area operation? (FAA-S-8081-7A)

a. Failure to perform, or improper performance of high and low reconnaissance.

b. Failure to track the selected approach path or to fly an acceptable approach angle and rate of closure.

c. Improper RPM control.

d. Inadequate planning to assure obstacle clearance during the approach or the departure.

e. Failure to consider emergency landing areas.

f. Failure to select a definite termination point during the high reconnaissance.

g. Failure to change the termination point if conditions so dictate.

h. Failure to consider effect of wind direction or speed, turbulence, or loss of effective translational lift during the approach.

i. Improper takeoff and climb technique for existing conditions.

C. Pinnacle/Platform Operation

1. Describe a pinnacle/platform operation.

A pinnacle is an area from which the surface drops away steeply on all sides. A ridgeline is a long area from which the surface drops away steeply on one or two sides, such as a bluff or precipice. The absence of obstacles does not necessarily lessen the difficulty of pinnacle or ridgeline operations. Updrafts, downdrafts, and turbulence, together with unsuitable terrain in which to make a forced landing, may still present extreme hazards.

2. What are the steps involved in performing a pinnacle/platform operation?

Approach and Landing

1. Begin with a high reconnaissance to collect as much information as possible about the conditions and terrain. This includes wind direction and velocity, obstructions that could cause turbulence, obstacles that affect the approach path and landing, forced landing areas, terrain, and any other factors that influence the approach and landing.

2. The high reconnaissance should be conducted from 500 feet AGL at a safe airspeed. The low reconnaissance should be used to confirm everything seen on the high reconnaissance. Also, to double-check the wind and turbulence conditions at the landing site.

3. The approach should be as shallow as possible unless otherwise dictated by obstructions or turbulent conditions. The approach should be made using ETL, favorable winds, and ground effect. If leeward downdrafts are encountered, the student may have to make an immediate go-around to avoid being forced into the rising terrain.

4. Throughout the approach, the student should evaluate the landing area for suitability.

Takeoff

1. Before takeoff, a ground reconnaissance is made to evaluate the area. This includes checking the wind direction and velocity, the terrain, and the best route of flight during the takeoff and departure.

2. A normal takeoff from hover should be conducted unless some obstacles exist. In this case, a maximum performance takeoff from the surface should be made to clear the obstacle.

3. During the departure, priority is given to gaining airspeed rather than altitude in order to facilitate an autorotation.

3. What are some of the standards expected of a student for a pinnacle/platform operation? (FAA-S-8081-16)

a. Exhibits knowledge of the elements related to pinnacle/platform operations.

b. Accomplishes a proper high and low reconnaissance.

c. Selects a suitable approach path, termination point, and departure path.

d. Tracks the selected approach path at an acceptable approach angle and rate of closure to the termination point.

e. Maintains RPM within normal limits.

f. Terminates at a hover or on the surface as conditions allow.

g. Accomplishes a proper ground reconnaissance.

h. Selects a suitable takeoff point, considers factors affecting takeoff and climb performance under various conditions.

4. What are some common student errors when performing a pinnacle/platform operation? (FAA-S-8081-7A)

a. Failure to perform, or improper performance of high and low reconnaissance.

b. Failure to track selected approach path or to fly an acceptable approach angle and rate of closure.

c. Improper RPM control.

d. Inadequate planning to assure obstacle clearance during approach or departure.

e. Failure to consider emergency landing areas.

f. Failure to select a definite termination point during the high reconnaissance.

g. Failure to change the termination point if conditions so dictate.

h. Failure to consider effect of wind direction or speed, turbulence, or loss of effective translational lift during the approach.

i. Improper takeoff and climb technique for existing conditions.

Helicopter Operations:
Airline Transport Pilot

Equipment Examination

1

A. Landing Gear

1. Describe how a typical skid-type landing gear will absorb a hard landing. (POH)

A spring and yield skid-type landing gear is used. Most hard landings will be absorbed by the gear's elastically. In an extremely hard landing, the struts will hinge up and outward as the center, cross tube yields (takes permanent set) to absorb the impact.

B. Powerplant and Transmission

1. Describe a turboshaft engine. (AC 65-12A)

Turboshaft engines are similar to turboprop engines. The power takeoff may be coupled directly to the engine turbine, or the shaft may be driven by a turbine of its own (free turbine) located in the exhaust stream.

2. Describe the free turbine. (AC 65-12A)

The free turbine rotates independently of engine's turbine.

3. Describe how the power is transferred from a turbine engine to the transmission.

A freewheeling unit is mounted within the engine accessory gearbox. Engine power is directed from the power take-off gear shaft to splines on the outer race shaft of the freewheeling unit. A sprag clutch assembly within the freewheeling unit engages the outer race shaft with the inner shaft. Power is then directed from the main output adapter on the freewheeling unit through the main drive shaft to the transmission.

4. How is the power transferred from the transmission to the tail rotor? (POH)

The tail rotor drive train is flexible in design to accommodate the movement of the tail boom during operation. The drive train is made up of eight individual drive shafts and five tail rotor driveshaft segments. The first two are steel and the remainders are aluminum alloy. There are nine laminated flexible couplings, requiring no lubrication, used to connect the individual shafts to each other and the tail rotor gearbox. The drive shafts are supported by seven hanger bearing assemblies.

C. Fuel System

1. Describe the fuel system for a typical helicopter with a turbine engine. (POH)

The fuel system incorporates a single, crash resistant, bladder type fuel cell located below and aft of the passenger seat. Installed with the fuel cell are two electrically operated boost pumps, lower and upper tank indicating units and an electrically operated sump drain valve.

D. Oil Systems

1. What is the primary purpose of oil jets in the transmission?

They lubricate planetary pinions and mast bearing, and spray the spiral bevel gear of the transmission.

2. What are the transmission lubricating system pressures? (POH)

Minimum .... 30 p.s.i.
Continuous .... 30–50 p.s.i.
Maximum .... 70 p.s.i.

3. How are metallic chips in the oil system detected? (POH)

The chip detector consists of a self-locking bayonet probe with a permanent magnet at the end. If metal particles become free in the oil, the magnet will attract the metal particles, allowing for inspection. If the chip detector is electric, when sufficient metal is attracted to complete the circuit between pole and ground, the appropriate light will illuminate.

4. How is the oil cooled? (AC 65-12A)

The oil cooler is either cylindrical or elliptical shaped and consists of a core enclosed in a double-walled shell. The core is built of copper or aluminum tubes with the tube ends formed to a hexagonal shape and joined together in the honeycomb effect. This allows the oil to flow through the spaces between the tubes while the cooling air passes through the tubes.

5. Where in the oil system is the oil temperature taken? (AC 65-12A)

The bulb is located so that it measures the temperature of the oil before it enters the engine's hot sections.

E. Hydraulic System

1. What are the basic components of a hydraulic system?

Hydraulic Fluid
Filters
Hydraulic Pump
Reservoir
Relief Valve
Accumulators
Actuators

2. What is the reason for using a liquid rather than a gas in the hydraulic system? (AC 65-15A)

Hydraulic system liquids are used primarily to transmit and distribute forces to various units to be actuated. Liquids are able to do this because they are almost incompressible. One of the most important properties of any hydraulic fluid is its viscosity.

3. **What are the different types of hydraulic fluids and how can they be identified?** (AC 65-15A)

Vegetable base hydraulic fluid (MIL-H-7644) is composed essentially of castor oil and alcohol. It has a pungent alcoholic odor and is generally dyed blue.

Mineral base hydraulic fluid (MIL-H-5606) is processed from petroleum. It has an odor similar to penetrating oil and is dyed red.

Phosphate ester base fluids (Skydrol® 500B-4, Skydrol® LD-4) are clear purple liquid. This type of fluid is a nonpetroleum base, fire-resistant, and formulated for use in large and jumbo jet transport aircraft.

4. **Why is it important to have a filter in the hydraulic system?** (AC 65-15A)

Filters provide adequate control of the contamination problem during all normal hydraulic system operations. A filter is a screening or straining device used to clean the hydraulic fluid, thus preventing foreign particles and contaminating substance from remaining in the system. If such objectionable material is not removed, it may cause the entire hydraulic system of the aircraft to fail through the breakdown or malfunctioning of a single unit of the system.

5. **What are some different types of hydraulic pumps?** (AC 65-15A)

Constant-delivery pump—Regardless of pump RPM there is a fixed or unvarying quantity of fluid through the outlet port during each revolution of the pump. Constant-delivery pumps are sometimes called constant-volume or fixed-delivery pumps.

Variable-delivery pump—A variable-delivery pump has a fluid output that is varied to meet the pressure demands of the system by varying its fluid output. The pump output is changed automatically by a pump compensator within the pump.

6. What are the two main types of reservoirs? (AC 65-15A)

In-line—This type has its own housing, is complete within itself, and is connected with other components in a system by tubing or hose.

Integral—This type has no housing of its own but is merely a space set aside within some major component to hold a supply of operational fluid. A familiar example of this type is the reserve fluid space found within most automobile brake master cylinders.

7. What is the purpose of the relief valve on a hydraulic system? (AC 65-15A)

A pressure relief valve is used to limit the amount of pressure being exerted on a confined liquid. This is necessary to prevent failure of components or rupture of hydraulic lines under excessive pressures.

8. What is the purpose of the accumulator? (AC 65-15A)

The accumulator is a steel sphere divided into two chambers by a synthetic rubber diaphragm. The upper chamber contains fluid at system pressure, while the lower chamber is charged with air. The function of an accumulator is to:

a. Dampen pressure surges in the hydraulic system caused by actuation of a unit and the effort of the pump to maintain pressure at a preset level.

b. Aid or supplement the power pump when several units are operating at once by supplying extra power from its "accumulated" or stored power.

c. Store power for the limited operation of a hydraulic unit when the pump is not operating.

d. Supply fluid under pressure to compensate for small internal or external (not desired) leaks witch would cause the system to cycle continuously by action of the pressure switches continually "kicking in."

9. What is the function of an actuator? (AC 65-15A)

An actuating cylinder transforms energy in the form of fluid pressure into mechanical force, or action, to perform work. It is used to impart linear powered motion to some moveable object or mechanism.

F. Electrical System

1. What is the difference between an alternator and a generator? (AC 65-9A)

An alternator supplies AC current and has a steady output at low power settings. A generator supplies DC current and does not work well at low engine RPM.

2. What is a starter-generator? (AC 65-15A)

Many gas turbine aircraft are equipped with starter-generator systems. These systems use a combination starter-generator, which operates as a starter motor to drive the engine during starting; and, after the engine has reached a self-sustaining speed, operates as a generator to supply the electrical system power.

3. What are the two most common types of batteries and how are they rated? (AC 65-9A)

Lead-acid and nickel-cadmium. The voltage of a lead-acid battery is determined by the number of cells connected in series to form the battery. One cell being rated at only 2 volts. A battery rated at 12 volts consists of six lead-acid cells connected in series.

4. Briefly explain how each type of battery works.
(AC 65-9A)

Lead-acid—The cells of a battery are connected in series. Each cell contains positive plates of lead peroxide, negative plates of spongy lead, and electrolyte (sulfuric acid and water). In discharging, the chemical energy stored in the battery is changed to electrical energy; in charging, the electrical energy supplied to the battery is changed to chemical energy and stored.

Nickel-cadmium — The positive plates are made from a porous plaque on which nickel-hydroxide has been deposited. The negative plates are made from similar plaques on which cadmium-hydroxide is deposited. When a charging current is applied to a nickel-cadmium battery, the negative plates lose oxygen and begin forming metallic cadmium. The active material of the positive plates, nickel-hydroxide, becomes more highly oxidized. The chemical action is reversed during discharge. The positive plates slowly give up oxygen, which is regained by the negative plates.

5. **What are some different types of circuit protection devices?** (AC 65-9A)

Fuses — A fuse is a strip of metal that will melt when current in excess of its carefully determined capacity flows through it. The fuse is installed in the circuit so that all the current in the circuit passes through it. In most cases, the strip of metal is made of an alloy of tin and bismuth.

Current limiters — A current limiter is a thin strip of copper and is primarily used to sectionalize an aircraft circuit.

Circuit breakers — A circuit breaker is designed to break the circuit and stop the current flow when the current exceeds a predetermined value. It is commonly used in place of a fuse and may sometimes eliminate the need for a switch. A circuit breaker differs from a fuse in that it "trips" to break the circuit and it may be reset, while a fuse melts and must be replaced.

Regulations 2

1. **What are the equipment requirements for VFR flight at night or VFR on the top for helicopters that are carrying passengers for hire?** (14 CFR 135.159)

   No person may operate an aircraft carrying passengers under VFR at night or under VFR over-the-top, unless it is equipped with —

   a. A gyroscopic rate-of-turn indicator except on the following aircraft:
      • Helicopters with a third attitude instrument system usable through flight attitudes of ±80 degrees of pitch and ±120 degrees of roll and installed in accordance with §29.1303(g) of this chapter.
   b. A slip skid indicator.
   c. A gyroscopic bank-and-pitch indicator.
   d. A gyroscopic direction indicator.
   e. A generator or generators able to supply all probable combinations of continuous in-flight electrical loads for required equipment and for recharging the battery.
   f. For night flights —
      • An anti-collision light system;
      • Instrument lights to make all instruments, switches, and gauges easily readable, the direct rays of which are shielded from the pilots' eyes; and
      • A flashlight having at least two size "D" cells or equivalent.

2. What are the equipment requirements for carrying passengers on an IFR flight for helicopters? (14 CFR 135.163)

No person may operate an aircraft under IFR, carrying passengers, unless it has —

a. A vertical speed indicator;

b. A free-air temperature indicator;

c. A heated pitot tube for each airspeed indicator;

d. A power failure warning device or vacuum indicator to show the power available for gyroscopic instruments from each power source;

e. An alternate source of static pressure for the altimeter and the airspeed and vertical speed indicators;

f. For a single-engine aircraft:

- Two independent electrical power generating sources each of which is able to supply all probable combinations of continuous in-flight electrical loads for required instruments and equipment; or

- In addition to the primary electrical power generating source, a standby battery or an alternate source of electric power that is capable of supplying 150% of the electrical loads of all required instruments and equipment necessary for safe emergency operation of the aircraft for at least one hour;

g. For multi-engine aircraft, at least two generators or alternators each of which is on a separate engine, of which any combination of one-half of the total number are rated sufficiently to supply the electrical loads of all required instruments and equipment necessary for safe emergency operation of the aircraft except that for multi-engine helicopters, the two required generators may be mounted on the main rotor drive train; and

h. Two independent sources of energy (with means of selecting either) of which at least one is an engine-driven pump or generator, each of which is able to drive all required gyroscopic instruments powered by, or to be powered by, that particular source and installed so that failure of one instrument or source, does not interfere with the energy supply to the remaining instruments or the other energy source unless, for single-engine aircraft in all cargo operations only, the rate of turn indicator has a source of energy separate from the bank and pitch and direction indicators. For the purpose of this paragraph, for multi-engine aircraft, each engine-driven source of energy must be on a different engine.

i. For the purpose of paragraph (f) of this section, a continuous in-flight electrical load includes one that draws current continuously during flight, such as radio equipment, electrically driven instruments, and lights, but does not include occasional intermittent loads.

3. What are the regulations regarding airborne thunderstorm detection equipment requirements? (14 CFR 135.173)

a. No person may operate an aircraft that has a passenger seating configuration, excluding any pilot seat, of 10 seats or more in passenger-carrying operations, except a helicopter operating under day VFR conditions, unless the aircraft is equipped with either approved thunderstorm detection equipment or approved airborne weather radar equipment.

b. No person may operate a helicopter that has a passenger seating configuration, excluding any pilot seat, of 10 seats or more in passenger-carrying operations, under night VFR when current weather reports indicate that thunderstorms or other potentially hazardous weather conditions that can be detected with airborne thunderstorm detection equipment may reasonably be expected along the route to be flown, unless the helicopter is equipped with either approved thunderstorm detection equipment or approved airborne weather radar equipment.

c. No person may begin a flight under IFR or night VFR conditions when current weather reports indicate that thunderstorms or other potentially hazardous weather conditions that can be detected with airborne thunderstorm detection equipment,

Continued

required by paragraph (a) or (b) of this section, may reasonably be expected along the route to be flown, unless the airborne thunderstorm detection equipment is in satisfactory operating condition.

d. If the airborne thunderstorm detection equipment becomes inoperative en route, the aircraft must be operated under the instructions and procedures specified for that event in the manual required by §135.21.

4. What are the performance requirements for helicopters carrying passengers for hire or in over-the-top or IFR conditions? (14 CFR 135.181)

a. Except as provided in paragraphs (b) and (c) of this section, no person may —

1. Operate a single-engine aircraft carrying passengers over-the-top; or

2. Operate a multiengine aircraft carrying passengers over-the-top or in IFR conditions at a weight that will not allow it to climb, with the critical engine inoperative, at least 50 feet a minute when operating at the MEAs of the route to be flown or 5,000 feet MSL, whichever is higher.

b. Notwithstanding the restrictions in paragraph (a)(2) of this section, multiengine helicopters carrying passengers offshore may conduct such operations in over-the-top or in IFR conditions at a weight that will allow the helicopter to climb at least 50 feet per minute with the critical engine inoperative when operating at the MEA of the route to be flown or 1,500 feet MSL, whichever is higher.

c. Without regard to paragraph (a) of this section, if the latest weather reports or forecasts, or any combination of them, indicate that the weather along the planned route (including takeoff and landing) allows flight under VFR under the ceiling (if a ceiling exists) and that the weather is forecast to remain so until at least 1 hour after the estimated time of arrival at the destination, a person may operate an aircraft over-the-top.

d. Without regard to paragraph (a) of this section, a person may operate an aircraft over-the-top under conditions allowing—
  - For multiengine aircraft, descent or continuance of the flight under VFR if its critical engine fails; or
  - For single-engine aircraft, descent under VFR if its engine fails.

5. **Under Part 135 rules, what does the helicopter have to be equipped with to fly over water?** (14 CFR 135.183)

No person may operate a land aircraft carrying passengers over water unless it is a helicopter equipped with helicopter flotation devices.

6. **What is the VFR minimum altitude for helicopters under Part 135?** (14 CFR 135.203)

Except when necessary for takeoff and landing, no person may operate under VFR a helicopter over a congested area at an altitude less than 300 feet above the surface.

7. **What are the VFR visibility requirements for helicopters under Part 135?** (14 CFR 135.205)

No person may operate a helicopter under VFR in Class G airspace at an altitude of 1,200 feet or less above the surface or within the lateral boundaries of the surface areas of Class B, Class C, Class D, or Class E airspace designated for an airport unless the visibility is at least 1/2 mile during th day or 1 mile at night.

8. **What are the helicopter surface reference requirements for VFR flight under Part 135?** (14 CFR 135.205)

No person may operate a helicopter under VFR unless that person has visual surface reference or, at night, visual surface light reference, sufficient to safely control the helicopter.

9. **What are the VFR fuel requirements for flight under Part 135?** (14 CFR 135.209)

   No person may begin a flight operation in a helicopter under VFR unless, considering wind and forecast weather conditions, it has enough fuel to fly to the first point of intended landing and, assuming normal cruising fuel consumption, to fly after that for at least 20 minutes.

10. **What are the IFR alternate airport requirements for helicopter flight under Part 135?** (14 CFR 135.233)

    a. Except as provided in paragraph (b) of this section, no person may operate an aircraft in IFR conditions unless it carries enough fuel (considering weather reports or forecasts or any combination of them) to:

    • Complete the flight to the first airport of intended landing;

    • Fly from that airport to the alternate airport; and

    • Fly after that for 30 minutes at normal cruising speed.

    b. Paragraph (a)(2) of this section does not apply if part 97 of this chapter prescribes a standard instrument approach procedure for the first airport of intended landing and, for at least one hour before and after the estimated time of arrival, the appropriate weather reports or forecasts, or any combination of them, indicate that —

    • The ceiling will be at least 1,500 feet above the lowest circling approach MDA; or

    • If a circling instrument approach is not authorized for the airport, the ceiling will be at least 1,500 feet above the lowest published minimum or 2,000 feet above the airport elevation, whichever is higher; and

    • Visibility for that airport is forecast to be at least three miles, or two miles more than the lowest applicable visibility minimums, whichever is the greater, for the instrument approach procedure to be used at the destination airport.

11. What are the operating limitations for icing conditions? (14 CFR 135.227)

No pilot may take off an aircraft that has frost, ice, or snow adhering to any rotor blade, propeller, windshield, wing, stabilizing or control surface, to a powerplant installation, or to an airspeed, altimeter, rate of climb, or flight attitude instrument system, except under the following conditions:

a. Takeoffs may be made with frost adhering to the wings, or stabilizing or control surfaces, if the frost has been polished to make it smooth.

b. Takeoffs may be made with frost under the wing in the area of the fuel tanks if authorized by the Administrator.

No pilot may fly a helicopter under IFR into known or forecast icing conditions or under VFR into known icing conditions unless it has been type certificated and appropriately equipped for operations in icing conditions.

12. To act as pilot-in-command of a helicopter during IFR operations under Part 135, what minimum experience is required? (14 CFR 135.243)

The pilot-in-command must hold at least a commercial pilot certificate with appropriate category and class ratings and if required, an appropriate type rating for that aircraft; 1,200 hours of flight time as a pilot, including:

a. 500 hours of cross-country flight time;

b. 100 hours of night time; and

c. 75 hours of actual or simulated instruments time, at least 50 of which were in actual flight.

d. Hold a helicopter instrument rating or ATP certificate with a category and class rating for that aircraft, not limited to VFR.

13. What are the second-in-command pilot qualifications for flight under Part 135? (14 CFR 135.245)

If the helicopter is operated under VFR the SIC needs to have at least a commercial pilot certificate with appropriate category and class rating. For VFR over-the-top or IFR flights the SIC must have a current instrument rating in the category and class of aircraft to be flown.

14. What are the pilot limitations for helicopter hospital emergency medical evacuation service (HEMES)? (14 CFR 135.271)

a. No certificate holder may assign any flight crewmember, and no flight crewmember may accept an assignment for flight time if that crewmember's total flight time in all commercial flight will exceed—

- 500 hours in any calendar quarter.
- 800 hours in any two consecutive calendar quarters.
- 1,400 hours in any calendar year.

b. No certificate holder may assign a helicopter flight crewmember, and no flight crewmember may accept an assignment, for hospital emergency medical evacuation service helicopter operations unless that assignment provides for at least 10 consecutive hours of rest immediately preceding reporting to the hospital for availability for flight time.

c. No flight crewmember may accrue more than 8 hours of flight time during any 24-consecutive hour period of a HEMES assignment, unless an emergency medical evacuation operation is prolonged. Each flight crewmember who exceeds the daily 8 hour flight time limitation in this paragraph must be relieved of the HEMES assignment immediately upon the completion of that emergency medical evacuation operation and must be given a rest period in compliance with paragraph (h) of this section.

d. Each flight crewmember must receive at least 8 consecutive hours of rest during any 24 consecutive hour period of a HEMES assignment. A flight crewmember must be relieved of the HEMES assignment if he or she has not or cannot receive at least 8 consecutive hours of rest during any 24 consecutive hour period of a HEMES assignment.

e. A HEMES assignment may not exceed 72 consecutive hours at the hospital.

f. An adequate place of rest must be provided at, or in close proximity to, the hospital at which the HEMES assignment is being performed.

g. No certificate holder may assign any other duties to a flight crewmember during a HEMES assignment.

h. Each pilot must be given a rest period upon completion of the HEMES assignment and prior to being assigned any further duty with the certificate holder of —

   • At least 12 consecutive hours for an assignment of less than 48 hours.

   • At least 16 consecutive hours for an assignment of more than 48 hours.

i. The certificate holder must provide each flight crewmember at least 13 rest periods of at least 24 consecutive hours each in each calendar quarter.

Appendix:
Maneuvers Tables

PTS Standards—Private and Commercial

Task	Private Standards	Commercial Standards
Vertical Takeoff to a Hover		
Heading	±10°	±5°
Altitude	±1/2 within 10 feet, above 10 feet, ±5 feet	±1/2 within 10 feet, above 10 feet, ±5 feet
Position	4 feet	2 feet
Surface Taxi		
Heading	±10°	±5°
Ground Track	±4 feet	±2 feet
Position	4 feet	2 feet
Hovering Maneuvers		
Heading	±10°	±5°
Altitude	±1/2 within 10 feet, above 10 feet, ±5 feet	±1/2 within 10 feet, above 10 feet, ±5 feet
Position	4 feet	2 feet
Slope Operations		
Heading	±10°	±5°
Normal Takeoff		
Airspeed	±10 KIAS	±5 KIAS
Max Performance Takeoff		
Airspeed	±10 KIAS	±5 KIAS
Normal Approach		
Termination Point	±4 feet	±2 feet
Steep Approach		
Termination Point	±4 feet	±2 feet
Shallow Approach—Running Landing		
Heading	±10°	±5°
Go-Around Procedure		
Airspeed	±10 KIAS	±5 KIAS
Straight and Level Flight		
Airspeed	±10 KIAS	±5 KIAS
Altitude	±100 feet	±50 feet
Heading	±10°	±5°
Level Turns		
Airspeed	±10 KIAS	±5 KIAS
Altitude	±100 feet	±50 feet
Heading	±10°	±5°
Normal Climbs and Descents		
Airspeed	±10 KIAS	±5 KIAS
Level Off Altitude	±100 feet	±50 feet
Heading	±10°	±5°
Rapid Deceleration (Quick Stop)		
Heading	±10°	±5°

Continued

PTS Standards—Private and Commercial *(continued)*

Task	Private Standards	Commercial Standards
Straight-In Autorotation		
Predetermined Spot	±100 feet	±50 feet
Airspeed	±5 KIAS	±5 KIAS
RPM	Normal limits	Normal limits
180-Degree Autorotation		
Predetermined Spot	±100 feet	±50 feet
Airspeed	±5 KIAS	±5 KIAS
RPM	Normal limits	Normal limits
Power Failure at Altitude (Hovering Autorotation)		
Heading	±10°	±5°
Touchdown	Minimum Sideward Movement	Minimum Sideward Movement
Touchdown	No Rearward Movement	No Rearward Movement
Power Failure at Altitude (Forced Landing)		
Airspeed	±10 KIAS	±5 KIAS
RPM	Normal limits	Normal limits
Settling With Power		
The student must thoroughly understand and recognize the settling with power conditions and be able to safely recover.		
Low Rotor RPM		
The student should be able to recognize and recover from low rotor RPM prior to reaching 90% RPM.		
Tail Rotor Failure		
RPM	Normal limits	Normal limits
Confined Area		
RPM	N/A	Normal limits
Approach Angle	N/A	No more than 15°
Hazard	N/A	Avoid conditions for settling with power
Pinnacle Operations		
RPM	N/A	Normal limits

Normal Maneuver Speeds for the R-22

Takeoff and Climb Airspeed .... 60 KIAS

Normal Cruise Airspeed (Training) .... 70 KIAS

Best Rate of Climb Airspeed .... 53 KIAS

Maximum Range Airspeed .... 83 KIAS

Autorotative Descent Airspeed .... 65 KIAS

Maximum Glide Airspeed (autorotations) .... 75 KIAS

Minimum Rate of Descent (autorotations) .... 53 KIAS

Hovering Altitude .... 3 feet

PTS Standards—Instrument

Task	Limitations
Departure Procedure	
Airspeed	±10 KIAS
Altitude	±100 feet
Heading	±10°
Holding Procedure	
Airspeed	±10 KIAS
Altitude	±100 feet
Heading	±10°
Straight and Level Flight	
Airspeed	±10 KIAS
Altitude	±100 feet
Heading	±10°
Change of Airspeed	
Heading	±10°
Angle of Bank (when turning)	±5°
Airspeed	±10 KIAS
Altitude	±100 feet
Constant Airspeed Climbs and Descents	
Specific Rate of Climb	±100 fpm
Heading	±10°
Angle of Bank (when turning)	±5°
Airspeed	±10 KIAS
Leveling Off	±100 feet
Timed Turns to Magnetic Compass Heading	
Altitude	±100 feet
Airspeed	±10 KIAS
Angle of Bank (when turning)	±5°
Roll Out on Specific Heading	±10°
Steep Turns	
Angle of Bank (when turning)	30°
Altitude	±100 feet
Airspeed	±10 KIAS
Angle of Bank (when turning)	±5°
Roll Out on Specific Heading	±10°
Intercepting and Tracking	
Airspeed	±10 KIAS
Altitude	±100 feet
Heading	±5°
CDI Indication	No more than 3/4 scale deflection or within 10° in case of RMI
DME arc	Maintains that arc within 1 NM

Continued

PTS Standards—Instrument *(continued)*

Task	Limitations
Non-Precision Approach	
Prior to Final Approach Segment:	
Altitude	±100 feet
Heading	±10°
CDI Indication	Less than full-scale deflection of the CDI or within 10° in the case of an RMI
Airspeed	±10 KIAS
While on the Final Approach Segment:	
CDI Indication	No more than 3/4 scale deflection or within 10° in case of RMI
Airspeed	±10 KIAS
MDA	Maintains the MDA when reached +100' / -0' to the MAP
Precision Approach	
Prior to Final Approach Segment:	
Altitude	±100 feet
Heading	±10°
Airspeed	±10 KIAS
While on the Final Approach Segment:	
CDI Indication	No more than 3/4 scale deflection of either the localizer or glide slope indications
Airspeed	±10 KIAS
DH	Avoids descent below the DH before initiating a missed approach procedure or transitioning to a normal landing approach
Missed Approach	
Recommended Airspeed	±10 KIAS
Heading, Course, or Bearing	±10°
Altitude	±100 feet
Circling Approach	
Upon reaching MDA:	
Altitude	+100' / -0'
Heading	A flight path that permits a normal landing on a runway at least 90° from the final approach course.

Notes

Notes